GENIUS BY CHOICE

Your unconventional A–Z handbook to enhance your learning process

Giulia S. Remondino

Copyright © 2020 by Giulia S. Remondino.

All rights reserved. No part of this book may be re-produced or used in any manner without written permission of the copyright owner except for the use of quotations in a book review. For more infor-mation, address: giulia@geniusin21days.co.uk.

First paperback edition July 2020

ISBN 978-1-8380704-6-5 (paperback)
ISBN 978-1-8380704-8-9 (ebook)

www.geniusbychoice.co.uk

Interior Design by FormattedBooks.com

*To my family, who know that my dream of being
an author dates back to some decades ago;
To Yaw, who is my greatest ally in my everyday life;
To my London team, who share big dreams with
me and make me better every day;
And to all the Instructors around the world, current and future:
being part of this exceptional team is one of my greatest blessings*

'The more you learn, the less you fear'
—Julian Barnes

Contents

PREFACE 11
FOREWORD by Luca Lorenzoni 13
HOW TO USE THIS BOOK 17
    Choice about what to read first 17
    Choice about where to read.. 18
    Choice about where to stop.. 18
    Choice about where to practise 19
    Choice about how to improve even more 20
    Who Am I and How Did This Book Come to Life?.................... 20

PART 0. PRIMING... 27

Chapter One: Welcome to Prime 29

Chapter Two: Dream Up... 31
    P for Prepare 31
    R for Read.. 32
    I for Internalise.. 32
    M for Memorise 33
    E for Express 33

PART I. PREPARE.. 37

Chapter Three: Motivation.. 39
    Killer no. 1: Setting Wrong Goals—the Law of +1 40
    Killer no. 2: Optimism—the Law of the Motivation Sheet 42
    Killer no. 3: Relying on Discipline—the Law of Leverage 45
    Killer no. 4: DIY mode—the Law of Accountability Partner.... 47
    Killer no. 5: Expecting Too Much—the Law of Input–Output .. 48
    Killer no. 6: Looking Back—the Law of the Blank Page 51

- Chapter Four: Time 53
  - Main mistakes 54
    - The two prisons we build 54
    - Planning based on dreams rather than facts 55
    - Being reactive rather than proactive 55
    - Having a break when you are exhausted 57
    - Not managing the unexpected 57
    - Planning day by day 58
  - Planning 59
    - The DESIRE Technique 59
      - D for Decide 59
      - E for Estimate 60
      - S for Scheduled 61
      - I for Investigate 61
      - R for Revisit 62
      - E for Ending 62
    - Ready-To-Do Map 64
  - Sticking to the plan 64
    - Reason One: Wrong Planning 65
    - Reason Two: Laziness 65
    - Reason Three: Wrong Estimation 65
    - Reason Four: Interruptions 66
    - Note to self: include some time to plan your strategy 69
- Chapter Five: Create Your Momentum 70
  - Your Study Sanctuary 70
    - Strategy one: go back in time 70
    - Strategy two: experiment 71
      - Music: yes or no 71
      - Light 71
      - Posture 72
  - Your Success Kit 73
    - Your Genius Journal 74
  - Stop Internal Distractions 74
  - Focus. Study. Pause. Repeat. 75
    - What affects your attention 76
      - Circadian Rhythms and Chronotype 76
      - Learning Styles 76
      - Eat, Sleep, Exercise. 77
      - Difficulty and Emotions 77

  How to increase your focus 77
  Study Cycles.. 78

PART II. READ 83

Chapter Six: Assessment 85
  What is ahead of you 92
   Focus.. 92
   Speed 92
   Strategy 93
   Retention 93

Chapter Seven: Strategy before Speed—the Five Boosters 94
  Booster One: Cover.. 95
  Booster Two: Preview 97
  Booster Three: Goal 98
  Booster Four: Questions.. 99
   What do I know?—Activating your foreknowledge 100
   What do I want to know?—Be like Sherlock 101
  Booster Five: Flow 102

Chapter Eight: When Your Goal Is to Understand 103
  Subvocalisation and Regressions 103
  Critical Reading 104
   Meet your Ally 104
   Highest Speed vs Perfect+1 Speed.. 105
   How to improve immediately.. 106
   Is slow better? 107
   After you have practised a bit… 107
   How to improve with the Jumping Pointer......................... 108

Chapter Nine: When Your Goal Is not to Understand 109
  Skimming.. 109
   How to improve your skimming ability.............................. 111
  Scanning 111
   How to improve your scanning skills.................................. 112

Chapter Ten: Remarks and Practice 113
  Reading fast in a technological world................................... 114
  Practice... 115

PART III. INTERNALISE 125

Chapter Eleven: Decoding and Understanding...................... 131
  Hourglass One: Read.. 133

Hourglass Two: Child 133
    'It's not your intelligence,... 134
      a)... it's your Lack of Focus!' 134
      b)... it's your Lack of Vocabulary!' 134
      c)... it's your Language!' 135
      d)...it's your Background Knowledge!................................ 135

Chapter Twelve: Processing 136
  Hourglass Three: Do I need it? 136
  Hourglass Four: Label 136
    What is a label? 137
  Hourglass Five: Keywords and details 139
    How can you find an effective label/keyword? 140
    Keywords, not key sentences. 142
    To be in the text, or not to be in the text. 143
  Hourglass Six: Next paragraph 144
  Hourglass Seven: Check and skim (after one hour of study) 145

Chapter Thirteen: Organising 148
  Hourglass Eight: Mind Maps 148
    Zoom In—Zoom Out. 149
    Why Mind Maps never worked on you 149
    How to create a Mind Map 151
      Ready. Steady. 151
      Go. 152
      Branches 152
      Contents of the Mind Map 155
      Visuals 157
    Where you can apply Mind Maps 161

PART IV. MEMORISE 165

Chapter Fourteen: Characteristics 167

Chapter Fifteen: The Velcro Technique 169
  Velcro One: Trigger 171
    What happens when you skip this step? 171
    How does this step work 171
    Mistakes you want to avoid 172
  Velcro Two: New Information 173
    What happens when you skip this step 173
    How does this step work 174
    Mistakes you want to avoid 174

- Velcro Three: PAV 175
  - What happens when you skip this step 175
  - How does this step work 175
    - Paradox 175
    - Action 176
    - Vividness 176
  - Mistakes you want to avoid 176
- Velcro Four: Lock 177
  - What happens when you skip this step 177
  - How does this step work 178
  - Mistakes you want to avoid 178
- Velcro Five: Visualise 178
  - What happens when you skip this step 179
  - How does this step work 179
  - Mistakes you want to avoid 180

Chapter Sixteen: Memory Palace—and Its Many Aliases 181
- Why It Should Work 181
- Why It Does Not Work 182
  - No Velcro 183
  - Panacea 184
- How It Will Work 185
  - How to Start 185
  - Heads up 187
    - Mind the triggers 187
    - I remembered some of it also without Velcro 187
    - How many objects 188
    - Not only rooms… 188
    - Using the same place y/n 190

Chapter Seventeen: Numbers (and Codes) 193
- The Phonetic System 194
  - Brick One: the sounds 194
  - Brick Two: the rules 196
    - Special letters 196
    - Doubles 197
    - Solutions 198
  - Brick Three: some practice 198
  - Brick Five: the hooks 200
  - Brick Six: Velcro Technique and having fun 203
  - Let's have some fun 204

How to remember lists of ten items: the Multiplier 205
    Alternative hooks with 'H' 205
    Alternative hooks with zero 205
    Verbal hooks 205
    Graphic hooks 206
One to five 208
Alphanumeric Codes and Symbols 208

Chapter Eighteen: Applications (Trigger–New Information) 211

Chapter Nineteen: Long-Term Memorisation 213
The evolution of Spaced Repetition: Timed Recalls 214
    Spaced Repetition—Y or N 214
    Why Recalls? 215
    Why Timed? 215
        The most important 216
        How precise with the timing? 217
        The main mistakes 217

PART V. EXPRESS 221

Chapter Twenty: Peak Performance 224
News Time 224
    Confirmation Bias and Internal Dialogue 225
    Managing the Bias 226
        Change the questions 226
        Substitute 228
Prep Time 231
Wait Time 231
    Dream on 231
        What people tend to do 231
        What you can do instead 232
        How to do it well 233
    Relax Productively 234
        What people tend to do 234
        What you can do instead 234
        If you really cannot get your mind off it 234
Showtime 235
    Energy first 235
        Breathe 235
        Body 236
    Relaxation then 236

> Breathe 237
> Get tenser and tenser 237

Chapter Twenty-One: Presentation Is Key 239
> Preparing 240
> > One goal, different strategies 240
> > The clearer the concept, the clearer the expression 241
> > > Clear Structure 242
> > > Clear Explanation 244
> > > Iceberg 245
> Presenting 246
> > Memory 246
> > Nerves 246
> > Becoming engaging 247

CONCLUSION 249
BEGINNING 249
YOUR A-Z HANDBOOK 253
ACKNOWLEDGEMENTS 255
REFERENCES 257

PREFACE

Welcome to Genius by Choice*!*

Before starting your journey, I would like you to focus your attention for one moment on why you have decided to read this book. Why would you like to improve your memory, reading skills or overall learning? This is something I always ask. 'Why improve your efficiency? Why now?'

It is not a question that stems solely from my curiosity. I will probably never even know your answer. But you asking this question of yourself will mark a difference: between your reading just another book that will become a faraway memory stored in a corner of your mind—or your making sure that you apply what you need to start enhancing your learning process.

When I have the chance to ask 'Why?' in person, people's answers may vary in the details, but they all contain a common thread.

No one wants to improve their memory or their reading speed in and of itself. Instead—for everyone I have spoken to—memorising and reading efficiently are tools with which to learn something new; a means to a more important end.

Learning a language in a month or two.

Studying a book to enhance your career.

Learning new skills to take on a new project.

Reading more books to enrich your mind.

Presenting confidently, in a way that leads people to take action.

When you type 'How to study better' into Google, 2.71 billion results (billion, with a 'b') pop up. It is normal for you to feel overwhelmed by possible solutions. You are never going to have the time to try them all and see which ones are the most effective.

At Genius in 21 Days, after training thousands and thousands of students in our centres, we have developed a unique recipe, one that puts the most advanced learning techniques together with an essential element to any learning programme: you. You, with your unique characteristics. You, with your unique cognitive profile. You, with your unique background and dreams.

No one has the same combination of characteristics as you do. And what is more important, these characteristics need to be understood and respected if you want to learn how to use the incredible potential of your brain. Any learning programme needs to be tailored to you like a bespoke piece of clothing.

This is the real problem with the relationship most people have with studying. The majority have spent their school and academic years trying to fit into clothes that were not meant for them, rather than finding someone who would fit the clothes to their unique characteristics.

At Genius in 21 Days we metaphorically make your bespoke clothes by tailoring the perfect method for you, thanks to our pre-assessment test and our 1-2-1 mentoring sessions. In these sessions your Mentor—acting like a PT for your brain—helps you to achieve your results and become autonomous with the method (you can access our free webinar from our website geniusin21days.co.uk).

While it is impossible for me to properly create your tailored learning method on paper, without having first assessed and analysed your cognitive profile, what I can do is help you find some clarity in the ocean of information that you may feel overwhelmed by (2.71 billion results, remember?).

There are some extremely effective techniques that are easy to share and, most importantly, are proven to work for everyone. They are our ABC, and you should learn them and apply them, because they will make your studying hours instantly more effective. After all, to become any kind of writer (novelist, poet, journalist, screenwriter, librettist...), the ABC is the point at which everyone needs to start. Genius by Choice *will walk you through the ABC, until you master it.*

Enjoy your journey—but, most importantly, enjoy the regained efficiency you will find, and the time you will be free to finally choose how to use.

FOREWORD
by Luca Lorenzoni

When Giulia asked me to write the foreword for *Genius by Choice*, I was incredibly enthusiastic about contributing. She is a person that holds great significance in my life. She is not only one of my best friends, but also a figure I hold in high esteem; both personally and professionally.

Our adventure together started on the 22nd November 2008, when she attended an event I was holding in Turin, Italy. She had just taken her Genius in 21 Days course, and had fatefully sat at my table during the lunch break. This was back during my days as an Instructor whilst managing my branch of Genius in 21 Days in Turin, and I would regularly enjoy lunch with the course attendees; however, it wasn't then that our friendship started.

Some months passed; after immediately flourishing from applying the learning techniques she had acquired from the course across various facets of her day-to-day life, she asked me to train her to become an Instructor herself. Of course I did not hesitate, knowing the tireless work ethic and enthusiasm Giulia had for learning, and within months she started working with Genius in 21 Days.

A few years later, there came a moment in which our company started to expand a lot and, since Giulia has an incredible passion for languages, when we made the decision to open a branch of Genius in the U.S.A., she was part of the task force gathered to scope out and launch this ambitious project.

While working on this expansion strategy, we had the opportunity to get to know each other better in our daily lives, and to face and overcome many challenges together along the journey. Smooth seas don't make good sailors, as the old adage goes!

We had meticulously planned every detail, vividly dreamt of the day in which she would receive her visa to work in the States, dedicated more than a year on this project, and finally the day arrived, where she had to go to the embassy to have the final interview for the permanent visa.

I remember the night before the day of reckoning was full of apprehension; I couldn't sleep in anticipation of the day in which our American dream would become a reality. But unfortunately (or luckily) the plan didn't come to fruition. The visa was rejected and our dream to bring our talents, our passion and our values to an Anglophone country disappeared in an instant.

It looked like there was no solution to alleviate this situation. But the same day, Giulia called me and explained she had no intention of giving up of that dream, and intended to evaluate opening a branch in London, which would be the first in the UK. Obviously, the immigration process would be much simpler compared to the United States, as London was still in the EU.

As soon as she told me about her idea, I said 'OK!'.

I must say that the merits Giulia has for opening Genius in 21 Days in the UK were (and continue to be) enormous! She stepped up to take the responsibility of managing not just a new centre, but a new country.

She is the living example of how perseverance and positivity in the face of adversity can transform something that initially doesn't go as planned, into something that exceeded your initial expectations.

From that moment on, our relationship became closer and deeper and we started working together, more in London than what we used to do together in Italy. I would often travel to the British capital to run some courses, and it was during this time that my professional relationship and friendship with Giulia continued to develop.

However, this foreword is not about the relationship we have built throughout the years, but about the high esteem I hold for her and for her numerous talents: her sweetness, her lucidity, her heart and her intelligence.

I think there is no better person to follow if you are committed to taking your learning results to the next level.

As has been proven across the annals of history, a leader is a person that leads by example, and Giulia does exactly this.

She started by anchoring Genius in 21 Days for a new country, and I am honoured to be part of her team as much as I am honoured that she is part of mine. Her team in London is made up of people that want to have an impact, making our world a better place, and helping people to feel better and overcome their perceived limits. I can't wait to be back in London; to hug all the wonderful London staff Giulia has assembled, because they are extraordinary people that enhance the lives of many others!

Enjoy this book—get the most out of it, study it, learn it. Applying these techniques may be the key to enhancing your learning and ultimately creating the life you want.

Luca Lorenzoni,
Founder of Genius in 21 Days

HOW TO USE THIS BOOK

Genius By Choice is meant for you, and as such I want you to experience it in your own personal way (in case the title did not give it away, I value the concept of freedom and choice very highly). There will be a lot of content, because I want to equip you with real, effective tools to increase your efficiency as a learner. But I am well aware that some people never finish the novels they start, let alone self-improvement books, and I do not want you to feel that pressure. Nor do I want you to miss what you most need from these pages.

So I have thought deeply about how to make your journey with this book as simple and effective as possible, and in this section I am going to show you how you can use it in its full power.

Choice about what to read first

This is not a book that you must necessarily read in order. Do not get me wrong: you *can* read it in order; and, knowing myself, I would probably do so. However, learning is supposed to be a creative process, enjoyable and fun (we will get to that soon), and so I have structured the book to allow you to feel free to jump from one section to another at your pleasure. Any time in which you require something that has been discussed before, you will find the reference to the chapters or passages that you need, in case you have not been through that part yet.

Start with Part 0, though, as it will give you an overview of all the phases of learning for you to keep in mind, and this will be helpful regardless of what subject you decide to tackle first.

Chapter 2—Dream up will help you to identify what areas to chiefly focus on, according to your needs. Tick the boxes at your pleasure and at the end of the book I will remind you to go back to those boxes and make sure you have found the answers you were looking for.

Choice about where to read

One thing that I love is to read before falling asleep. However, as you can imagine, while some books are perfect for that purpose, there are others that I would prefer to make notes on or practise with. This book is a mixture of the two. There will be some parts that you can read on your commute or in bed, while there will be others for which it would be better to sit at your desk, so as to practise your new skill.

In order to give you the flexibility of reading it at any time you wish, wherever you are, and to save you from the disappointment of being in bed and needing to stand up and write all of a sudden, under each Chapter title you will find written 'Desk is better' or 'Bed is fine', so you can act accordingly.

Choice about where to stop

Probably most people would love to be able to snap their fingers and become more efficient, but these techniques are no instant fix (sorry if that is what you were expecting…). You will need to apply them to allow them to work their magic, and some of them will come easier than others.

I have some good news for you, though. Almost all the techniques can be tackled in layers.

The first layer is what I call the 'No Effort' layer. This means that just by applying what you read, without any practice, you will already see great improvement (and at times already feel like a 'Genius').

The second layer is what I call the 'Easy Peasy' layer. This requires you to invest a couple of minutes to write something down in your Genius Journal or apply what I am teaching you, but demands no particular mental effort (we'll get to the Genius Journal soon).

The third layer is what I call the 'Road to Mastery' layer. This involves those exercises or adjustments that may require some investment of time and effort on your part, but that can help you raise the bar even more.

According to how much you need that specific technique, you can choose whether to stop at the No Effort or Easy Peasy layers or invest some of your time to apply the Road to Mastery layer.

If you are struggling to find time to invest, then start from the No Effort and Easy Peasy layers. This will already allow you to be faster at learning, and you can choose to reinvest the time to save to practise the Road to Mastery layer, in order to be even more efficient further down the line.

From Part One onward, under each subheading you will find the name of the layer, so that you can choose whether to read it or save it for later.

Choice about where to practise

Recently I heard the expression 'high-stakes practice and low-stakes practice'. Whenever you practise any of the tools that I am teaching you in this book, there will be low-stakes and high-stakes practice opportunities. The low-stakes practice happens when you do not have much to be won or lost, so you can allow yourself to dare more. The high-stakes practice happens when there is a lot to lose, so your mind will find it harder to run risks.

As you can imagine, practising first in low-stakes scenarios will help you to increase your level of confidence with the new technique before applying it in the real world.

This is why after each section you will find a line like this:

Words: 123 *Time (in seconds):* _____

This will let you know how many words you have just read, as well as giving you the opportunity to write down how long it took you to read them. Until you get to Chapter Eight, you can ignore this line as if it was not there, but in that chapter you will see how you can use this in order to improve your reading efficiency in a low-stakes environment.

Choice about how to improve even more

I realise the content of this book is rich, and I have debated for a while about splitting it into more books or keeping it all together. I have chosen the latter because I want you to have all the tools you need, now.

However, should you feel overwhelmed—or if you would like to understand how to apply some of these techniques better, and how to personalise your method through Genius in 21 Days—we are here for you. By purchasing this book, you are eligible to receive a special gift: simply go to geniusbychoice.co.uk/gift to claim it!

Who Am I and How Did This Book Come to Life?

Let me start by telling my story. Not my *whole* story, only the parts in which I decided to become an Instructor with Genius in 21 Days, and then write *Genius by Choice*—so you can understand why I will help you become a Genius.

In 2008 I finished secondary school and needed to choose what to do next.

It was a real dilemma. I wanted to do something that would positively impact the world, and at the same time really make use of my potential. The functioning of our brain had always fascinated me, as had the discovery of new cultures.

When choosing from all the possible paths, I was torn between pursuing my curiosity to discover how we work internally, or continuing the work I had started as a sixteen-year-old exchange student in China for a year, which focused on exploring how other parts of the world reason and think. Should I study Neuroscience or International Relations? Eventually, I chose the latter.

However, a few months into my degree I realised that, by following that path, I wouldn't be able to make the kind of impact I wanted; one that was more aligned with my talents and passions.

Everyone has their aha moment. I still remember mine.

One day a diplomat came to our university to be interviewed. His face was so sad and disillusioned when he told us: 'Inside four walls we create perfect solutions that will never be applied outside.'

This resonated with the impression I had felt in those first months, and I was not willing to experience that sense of powerlessness I had seen in his eyes. I wanted to have a real impact—and find my own way to do it by living an amazing life.

I made a list of the three most important things to me. This is what I wrote: I want to leave a mark, I want to meet a lot of different people, and I want to travel and see the world.

A few months before, I had come across a memory techniques and speed-reading course, which was the embryonic stage of what would later become Genius in 21 Days; I had taken it and had achieved amazing results, far beyond the excellent ones I had attained in my studies previously.

I realised how this course could be the answer I had been searching for. I had loved it; I believed in the lasting impact it could have on whoever took it; it would allow me to interact with people daily and help them achieve extraordinary results by overcoming their own limits; and, who knows, maybe also travel the world.

I took a leap, asked my Instructor Luca Lorenzoni to train me to be able to open my own centre, and here I am. Between 2009 and 2020, a lot of things have happened.

To complete my training to become an Instructor, I undertook work experience in several Italian cities, which allowed me to adapt the course to very different kinds of audiences (it is incredible how culture may vary even in different regions of the same country).

Upon qualifying as an Instructor, I moved to London to open the UK market and start my own centre. I realised I was faced with a new challenge: that of adapting the course to the British culture without losing its effectiveness and spirit. The training I had been through in the previous years provided me with everything I needed to succeed at this, and I can only be grateful to those who trained me. They had not just taught me technical skills but helped me bring out those talents that I had inside; especially Luca Lorenzoni: founder of Genius in 21 Days, extraordinary mentor and now also one of my dearest friends.

What is wonderful about working in Genius in 21 Days is that when you are part of a team of fifty people who, in different parts of the world, are focused on making a service better and better, you can really work as a team to move forward much faster.

Thanks to this, Genius in 21 Days evolved from being a memory techniques and speed-reading course to becoming the first ever course specialised in helping people fall in love with learning again specialised in helping people fall in love with learning again through our unique tailoring process.

Learning should be fun and increase your confidence, but this is not always the case. The only way to put things back in their natural place is to discover your unique characteristics as a learner and to create your own tailored learning method.

Our method has received significant praise. The thousands of certified testimonials that our clients have written describing extraordinary results have started creating buzz in Italy. This has led to partnerships being established with important Italian institutions and scientists who are now carrying out specific research on the Genius method.

In 2018, there was a moment in which I realised that extraordinary was not good enough anymore, not for me at least (this is a mindset that you will recurrently find in our company across the globe), and I promised myself that every month I would make the course even better. I changed the way we delivered certain parts; I improved some of the content; and, thanks to the help of my London team—who supported me in my adventure of improving what already appeared perfect—I can say that the course we are delivering now is on another level compared to almost two years ago. I love it when old clients come to visit us during a course (one of the services we give is the possibility to retake the course in the future for free) and regardless of whether the course is being held in our office or online, they all say the same thing: 'The course was amazing when I took it some months ago, but now it is Genius 2.0'.

And who knows what the future holds for my team and me.

What I do know is that those teenage dreams—of making a difference in individuals' lives, of interacting with people daily and of travelling the world—are all a reality now. Those, plus a lot more dreams and desires that popped up along the journey. With the same dedication and passion I have put in to making them come true for me, I will provide you with all the tools you need to do the same for yourself.

The main message I want to convey is that you do not need to wait for something to be broken to fix it, as there is no limit to improvement. We are not perfect, and we will never be, as a company and as human beings; but each day we make sure we are closer to it than the one before. If you apply this same mentality while reading this book, the kind of results you are going to achieve will surprise you and supersede all your expectations.

There are many reasons why I decided to write this book. In 2019, I ran courses in Ghana to open up the African market and worked with people all over the world who travelled to London to take part in the programme. This fuelled my mission even more. I want as many people as possible to achieve the results that our clients achieve in London and in our Genius centres in Italy, Switzerland, the US and Spain. To be honest, what motivates me the most are not the results themselves. The results you can achieve mean something only compared to your own standard. What really moves me and drives me is to think about all those people who have learned (and will learn) how to do something that they previously thought impossible; because, when this happens, the look in their eyes changes and it is clear that a new perspective has opened up for them.

Another reason why I have decided to write this book, which I have wanted to write for some time now, is linked to the 2020 coronavirus situation. If we were solely reliant on running our courses live and in person, this would not be possible anymore; and so, again, we have had to reinvent ourselves. Consequently, a lot of barriers have been removed. We have started holding our courses online, where they have proven as interactive, as effective and as impactful as when held live. This now allows us to get in touch with many people who we would not have been able to connect with before.

When I saw people from all over the world attending our course on our online platform, I realised that there was no time to waste. The whole world needs to know the Genius method. So I started writing.

I cannot promise that reading a book will give you the same results that you would have by taking Genius in 21 Days (I am pretty sure it will not), but what I want for you is to start having a peek at your potential. Apply everything you can, and you will see your learning improve at a pace that you thought impossible before.

Words: 1,541   *Time (in seconds): _____*

PART 0.
PRIMING

CHAPTER ONE

Welcome to Prime

[Bed is fine]

Learning is a fascinating subject, indispensable for survival and evolution and yet never taught at school. The focus of the education system has traditionally been to teach subjects (*what*), but very few subjects have ever been taught *how* to study (if not for some sporadic cases, usually initiated by proactive teachers). I have no intention of opening any debate here; what I want you to focus on is the fact that if you do not know *how* to study, it will be hard to do it as effectively as you can. Someone could live with that and not really mind, but I want you to think about how pervasive learning is in your everyday life. Whether you need to remember a pin code or embark on an academic journey, learn how to cook a new dish or read the latest article on your favourite subject, speak a new language or understand how the latest update of your phone works, you cannot get by without learning. It is surely one of those life skills that you will use daily and that will make or break your results.

In this book we will focus on the active learning process that you put in place to acquire new knowledge. But first I have a question for you: what is learning? I do not want you to get philosophical, but I would like you to spend a few seconds thinking about it. As I do believe that one of the problems people encounter while learning comes from the fact that they are not aware of what steps one must include in their learning process in order for it to be effective.

So, how would you break down the learning process?

What are the stages that you think you need to include when you want to learn anything?

Done?

You may be wanting to learn a new language, prepare for a presentation, study for an exam or just read for your own pleasure. Regardless of the subject you are studying, learning must go through five stages. The only exception is when you are not 'studying' something but simply applying one or two of the steps, which could happen when, for example, you want to 'read' a book but not remember its content. Besides these exceptions, learning consists of our acquiring information from external sources, processing it inside our brain, retaining what we need and then using that information.

To simplify, we can split it into five phases, which are what the Genius PRIME Method takes its name from.

Preparation
Reading
Internalising
Memory
Expression

Throughout the book, you will be able to read about and become a master at each of these phases. But in order to get started, you first need to get ready (as you will see in the first phase), so read on to find an interesting exercise for you.

Words: 477   *Time (in seconds):* _____

CHAPTER TWO

Dream Up

[Desk is better, but bed is fine if you have a pencil]

What I will now ask you to do is to take a moment to think about what you would like to do with the techniques and tools that you are about to learn.

In the section in the introduction on 'how to read this book'—if you have skipped it, I'd advise to go back as it will give some interesting insight on how to get the most out of this text—you will see that I have made it as simple as possible for you to choose how to do so: you can either read it in order, or you can jump to the parts that you are more interested in first and then go back and read the rest after.

What you will find below is a collection of the most common questions I get asked about learning, arranged according to the part of the book you can find the answer in. No matter how you choose to proceed with your reading, I would advise you to tick all the questions that you would like answered, so that at the end of the book you can go back to this page (I will remind you, do not worry) and check you have not missed anything.

P for Prepare

- How can I prevent becoming demotivated during my preparation?
- How can I increase my motivation when I need to start preparing for an exam?

- How can I not be stressed while studying?
- Which background music is better when studying?
- If I like spending time in nature, what is productive for me?
- When I study, my mind keeps wandering. How can I stop getting distracted?
- How can I be more focused while studying?
- How can I have fun while learning?
- How can I manage my time effectively?
- How can I be more disciplined?

R for Read

- If I am a slow reader, what can I do?
- How can I be more focused while reading?
- Is there an exercise I can do to improve my reading speed?
- How can I read emails more quickly?
- Are there different strategies for reading different types of texts?
- How can I use speed-reading techniques on my computer?
- How can I read faster and still understand what I am reading?
- When reading, my eyes get tired: can I do anything about it?

I for Internalise

- How can I organise concepts effectively?
- What is the best way to highlight important points of a text?
- How can I understand complicated topics better?
- How can I know if I have understood what I have read?
- What is the most effective way to take notes?
- Is there a strategy to note down ideas effectively?
- Why do I feel I know details but then struggle to see the global picture?
- How can I learn concepts without reciting them word by word?

M for Memorise

- I heard about the memory palace, is it a technique worth exploring?
- How can I remember things forever?
- How can I remember people's names?
- Why do I think I know stuff but then get lost when I am asked a question?
- How can I remember numbers?
- How can I remember all the things I need to know for an exam?
- How can I memorise a list of items?
- If I can remember everything I want to, won't my mind be overfull?

E for Express

- How can I be relaxed during an exam?
- Is visualising before an exam good?
- How can I be relaxed while waiting for my exam results?
- How can I boost my confidence while presenting?
- I get stressed if I need to speak in front of someone: is there a way to calm my nerves?
- How can I organise ideas when expressing them?
- How can I structure my thoughts clearly when expressing them?
- How can I improve my public-speaking abilities?

Now that you have selected the main aspects you would like to work on, I need you to keep in mind something that will make a huge difference whenever you need to learn anything. It is a concept that has become popular thanks to Dr. Carol Dweck, PhD, through her book *Mindset*—in which she explains that there are two kinds of mindset we can have: fixed and growth.

In very simple terms, a fixed mindset is present when you believe that if you were born with x amount of a certain skill, you will die with the same amount. Have you ever told yourself 'This is who I am', or 'I am not gifted at languages', 'I am a slow reader' and so on? All of us may be able to spot some areas in which we have a fixed mindset, and those are the areas in which we feel more stressed when challenged; because, if our skill cannot really improve, every challenge becomes an opportunity to show that it is enough. This raises the stakes immensely.

A growth mindset is present when you believe, regardless of whether you are already good at something or not, that you can always improve. This will lead you to look for feedback so that you can become better, rather than avoiding it to protect your ego.

Unfortunately, most of us have been raised with a fixed mindset in one area or another. Have you ever been told 'Forget about this, it's not for you', or 'Why don't you study this instead? You are more gifted'?

Acknowledging this will make an immeasurable difference in your results. Any skill can be improved, more and more studies confirm it. Will you become the world champion at that skill that you do not have at all right now? Hardly so. But the level of improvement you can achieve will change everything, and will make you the champion in *your* world.

Every time you tell yourself you are amazing or terrible at something, ask yourself: What if I could improve? And let your mind find an answer for this. You will see your results transform.

Words: 1,037   *Time (in seconds):* _____

PART I. PREPARE

This is the most underestimated phase of learning: the phase that you skip if you are in a rush; and which, even when you have all the time in the world, you try to get over with as soon as possible because a voice says 'Let me get to what I *really* need to do to learn these things.'

I hate to break it to you, but Preparation is also *the* phase that will define whether you will achieve your goal, how quickly, and at what standard.

Without the mastery of this phase, you will find yourself wasting time and energy: not achieving the result that you would like and becoming extremely frustrated.

Have you ever postponed studying until you found yourself doing everything at the last minute? It comes from wrong Preparation.

Have you ever felt unmotivated when studying? It comes from wrong Preparation.

Have you ever found yourself studying more than you actually needed to, hence wasting a lot of time? It comes from wrong Preparation.

Have you ever lost focus while studying? A big chunk of this comes from wrong Preparation.

So, getting your Preparation right will affect your results immensely. Are you ready to start?

First of all, what is Preparation? Technically it means to get ready, but ready for what? And how?

Preparation includes four fundamental steps: motivation, time management, strategy and creating your momentum. (Not so sure you still want to underestimate it, right...?)

We will analyse the four aspects and begin work on each of them immediately.

Words: 254   Time (in seconds): _____

CHAPTER THREE

Motivation

[Bed is fine]

Motivation is one of the main factors that will define whether you will be disciplined enough to persist until you reach your goal or not.

However, it is often thought of as an element that you have no power over; either you have it or you do not. For some goals you will be motivated, for others you will not. At times believing that your motivation depends on your chosen goal rather than on yourself may be tempting, but it is not what will help you make sure your targets will be met.

Motivation tends to be considered as a hard-to-grasp factor; and when something is hard to grasp, we resign ourselves to the fact that we will not have control over it.

What if I told you that, to an expert eye, motivation is anything but hard-to-grasp, and can actually be divided into some easy to follow steps?

In this part, I am going to unravel the secrets to keeping your motivation up and high, by explaining the six killers of motivation and the hacks to beat them.

Before you read all about the killers of your motivation, I would like you to place your attention on the difference in drive and focus you feel when you are motivated by an external force, as opposed to when you are driven by something inside you that wants to grow, become better, improve or evolve.

Too often we have been used to relying on external stimuli to pursue our growth. I am not saying that this is a problem in itself—there may be times when it is thanks to this external force that we overcome fears that have held us back—however this book wants to take you on a journey that will not only enhance your abilities as a learner, but will also remind you that the strongest force you have comes from the inside. Once you allow yourself to remove your fears, it is then you can listen to what you really want, and can feel free to pursue it, strengthened by all the tools and skills you are aware you have.

Some of the killers and hacks will rely on your extrinsic motivation, others on your intrinsic; but you will see that, the more you acknowledge the steps you are taking, then more your intrinsic motivation will start prevailing.

Will there be times in which you may use a strategy that leverages your extrinsic motivation because you cannot find your intrinsic one? Sure. But they will become rare exceptions.

Words: 426   Time (in seconds): _____

Killer no. 1: Setting Wrong Goals—the Law of +1

{No effort layer}

How many times have you heard you should set a goal because 'you cannot hit a target you cannot see'? Still, it is easier said than done.

At times you know a goal will be pretty easy to achieve, so you are confident it is going to go well; but then what happens? You start postponing the actions you need to take, knowing that there is still time. Your mind (like everyone else's) has a lazy side that will seize any opportunity not to do. When your mind recognises that a task is too easy, it sits comfortably, like the hare in the famous fable. And then you will find yourself trying to catch up at the last minute, which may not leave you enough time to get everything done properly. So aiming low doesn't really work.

Let's see what happens when you aim high.

Aiming higher should make your goals more achievable, because if anything goes wrong, you will still be achieving something anyway (that's what they say, right?), but this strategy also never seems to work. The reason is this. For the first two days you take all the actions that you had planned. Then a hiccup occurs: you need to skip a day. You tell yourself you will catch up the following day. You will wake up extremely motivated to catch up, but you now need to do all the things you had planned for day four plus all the ones you did not do on day three. Your mind already thought it was too ambitious a goal when you set it, and now that thought is proving right. You find yourself behind, trying to play catch up. This becomes draining, and a voice inside keeps reminding you that you knew already that it would have been too hard for you. You start doing less instead of more.

When you believe something is too hard for you, you will tend not to face it, as in your mind it is much better to fail at something because of laziness than because of inability. Rather than putting in extreme effort and failing, our mind prefers not to do anything at all (and still fail).

So what is the solution?

The key is in setting a goal that is balanced: not too easy, not too hard. How do you do that? The answer is in the +1.

Ask yourself what you are one hundred per cent sure you will be able to achieve, then add one—thus setting a goal that is slightly higher than that one hundred per cent.

How many push ups are you sure you can do? Ten. Then your goal will be eleven. Not twenty, eleven. And from eleven you will grow, one push up at a time.

How many foreign words can you study in thirty minutes? Thirty. Then your goal will be thirty-one. Not fifty, thirty-one. And from thirty-one you will grow, one word at a time.

How many days will it take you to prepare for that exam? Fifteen. Then your goal will be to prepare for it in fourteen days. Not in ten, in fourteen. And then from fourteen you will become faster and faster and be able to do it in much less.

When you choose your goal, ask yourself: What am I one hundred per cent sure I can do? Then add one.

A final question before moving to the next step. At times the goal is 'forced' upon you by the outside and you cannot choose it: in that case, what do you do?

If the goal is too easy, make it challenging: by asking yourself to do something in a new way, or to do something that has never been done before. This will make it more enjoyable and stimulating.

If it is too hard, break it down into chunks, and make sure each chunk follows the +1 rule.

Words: 655 *Time (in seconds): _____*

Killer no. 2: Optimism—the Law of the Motivation Sheet

{Easy Peasy layer}

I will never be able to stress it enough: relying on your strong motivation to last forever is one of the main killers to your motivation itself; the reason being that, if you are over-optimistic, your laziness will find you unarmed. This does not mean that you should not be motivated anymore, but that you should know yourself and be prepared. Over-optimism leads you to underestimate the challenges; motivation leads you to do everything to be prepared to face them.

I have heard many people suggest that one of the keys to getting out of a moment of laziness is to think about the reasons why you wanted to achieve that goal in the first place. This strategy comes from logical intuition, but at the same time needs to be adjusted in order to really be effective. Let's see them both.

One of the factors affecting your motivation is indeed awareness of the reasons why you want to achieve your goal; and it is true that the more you connect with those reasons the more motivated you will be. It is interesting to note that the word motivation comes from motive, which means 'reason', and -ation, the suffix for 'action'. And if we go even further back, motive comes from the Latin word *motus*, which means 'movement'. Your reasons are what moves you to take certain actions, so focusing on them when you are stuck—so that you can *move* again—makes perfect sense.

There is only one problem with this strategy, which is that it is not always easy when you are having a lazy day to remember why you wanted to take those actions in the first place. All those reasons that seemed so clear when you set your goal are now blurry and slip your mind.

This is because the moment in which you should think about your motivations is that in which you are down, yet the only moment in which you are able to do so is when you are up. To solve this conundrum, there is a simple but effective strategy—the Motivation Sheet.

When you set your goal (when the reasons are still very clear), take a page (or a note on your phone, or your Genius Journal) and list why you want to achieve it. You need to be very thorough, and the best way to do it is by digging as much as you can to find all the reasons that move you. This is not the moment to be enlightened or polite. This is the moment to be effective. Writing reasons such as 'because I want to bring out the best part of myself' can work only if you really believe it and if it is not the only item on your list. Make sure your Motivation Sheet includes:

- At least thirty reasons
- Reasons based on both what you want to get and what you want to avoid ('I want to feel proud of myself'; 'I do not want to be the last'): think about the good things that will happen if you succeed and the bad consequences there will be should you fail
- Reasons based around both yourself and others ('I want to feel proud of myself'; 'I want my parents to be proud of me')

If you cannot get to thirty reasons, pick the ones you feel as the strongest and ask yourself 'Why is this reason so important for me?'

This will allow you to go deeper and find even more effective reasons to note down.

The effectiveness of the Motivation Sheet is amazing (and at times even surprising). When you feel unmotivated, all you have to do is to re-read that list: there will be at least one item that triggers your motivation and pushes you to take action.

Once I was working with a girl who had to take the final exam for her degree, but she hated university and she could not study at all. She told me: 'Giulia, I cannot find any reason for my Motivation Sheet.' I replied: 'Well, in that case do not take that exam.' She looked at me with a puzzled look and said: 'I cannot not take it. My parents would be so disappointed!' 'You see,' I replied. 'You already found one reason.'

She argued: 'Yes, but I cannot find any other, I'll never get to thirty'. At that point, I suggested she take that one reason, which was enough for her to push herself to study, and focus on why she did not want her parents to be disappointed. She did so; she came up with many more than thirty reasons; and she graduated. As I say, this is not the moment to be enlightened. I did not work with her on the fact that she was moving because of an external, negative leverage. In that moment, that was all she had. And it worked.

So note down all the reasons you have, and—if you really do this exercise well—all you will need is to look at this list in order to get back on track and start acting.

Words: 857   Time (in seconds): _____

Killer no. 3: Relying on Discipline—the Law of Leverage

{Easy Peasy layer}

Even for the most disciplined of you, there might come the day in which that sofa seems really inviting. I have seen a lot of people trying to fight the sofa, pooling all their strength to resist the temptation, but the reality is that you can only keep the wolf from the door for a while. Instead it works much better if you, rather than fighting your laziness, can learn to tame it. It is the Law of Leverage that allows you to do this.

As human beings, there are two main kinds of external leverage that move us in taking action towards our goals. On one side, we seek pleasure; on the other side, we want to avoid pain. Have you ever heard of the carrot and the stick? You need to learn how to use metaphorical carrots and sticks for yourself.

I would like to tell you that carrots are enough; but, when laziness kicks in, sticks will tend to be more effective.

So what will your carrots and sticks be?

Your stick will be a 'good punishment' you give yourself if you do not take the actions you were supposed to take that day. Let me be clear on what a 'good punishment' is. It needs to be something that is painful yet good for you; something that will not harm you. (Once a client said that her punishment would be not to eat the following day: no, this is not a 'good punishment'.) A 'good punishment' is something that you do not want to do but that you will have to do if you do not take the daily actions you have planned. You can phrase it as 'If I do not do what I have planned, I will have to...'. In all the years I have been training people, the most effective punishment I have found is when people choose to pay someone in case they do not do what they should. It is a great punishment: because no one wants to pay money as a fee for their laziness, while for the wealthiest there will also come a threshold where you are not willing to pay money simply as a consequence of being lazy. For some people it may be £5, for others £50, for others £1,000. But sooner or later you will hit that threshold where your mind will tell you 'Rather than paying that amount for nothing, just do what you have to, it's less painful.' Your goal will be not to pay the fee.

There are three rules you need to follow to make the 'good punishment' effective. The first is that if you do not take your actions you must pay the fee. This should be obvious, but my question is: have you ever cheated while playing solitaire? Most people have, you are not alone. But if you want to succeed you need to start recognising the tricks that your mind plays on you, in order to ensure that you know how to manage them. In the next paragraph, we are going to see how to make sure that you do pay your fee when you have to, even if your extrinsic motivation is still stronger than your intrinsic one.

The second rule is that once the fee is paid there is no time for guilt or recrimination. You have paid your fee; you are free to move on and achieve your goal. Very often not doing what you should brings with it a sense of guilt, which lowers your energy and motivation. Paying your fee frees you from that. You do not owe anything to anyone; you can move on and achieve your goal.

The third rule is something I have already mentioned that I want to make doubly sure you have understood. You do not pay the fee if you do not achieve your daily goal, but *if you do not do your daily action*. There is a big difference between input and output, and we are going to discuss it in law no. 5. But for now just remember that what you pay a fee for is not not achieving your goal, but not doing what you had planned to do in order to achieve it.

Enough with the stick, let's move on to the carrot.

Having something to look forward to will also help you bring out your energy and determination in the darkest days. And I have some good news for you: you will have two rewards, not just one.

The first reward will be a big one that you will be giving yourself if you achieve your medium-term goal. Let's say you want to learn 2,000 words of a language in two months. If you achieve your goal, you will treat yourself with a trip to a country where they speak that language, or with a day at a spa. The reward does not necessarily need to be related to the goal, but it needs to be a treat that you will allow yourself as an extra reward besides the satisfaction of having achieved your goal.

The second reward will be a small, short-term one that you set for the end of your daily study session. It could be a TV series episode, a sweet treat, a nice meal out, a walk in the park—anything that will keep your mind alert by giving you something to look forward to. You will notice your attention increasing immediately, and the nice thing is that the reward can change daily according to what you desire that day!

Words: 933   Time (in seconds): _____

Killer no. 4: DIY mode—the Law of Accountability Partner

{Easy Peasy layer}

When a goal does not have a real deadline, regardless of how important it may be for our life, most of us will tend to favour laziness over consistency. This concept by now should be pretty clear. In the last paragraph we explored the Law of Leverage, and I mentioned that I would show you a way to make sure you would stop cheating yourself.

I would like to tell you that there is a magic wand that will remove any temptation to cheat from your life, but there is not, and mastering willpower to that level may take some time. The good news is that there is a shortcut you can take, which—if used properly—can be extremely effective.

This strategy consists of finding an accountability partner: a 'buddy', a person who will check on you day by day to make sure you have done what you said you would. When you have not, your buddy will mandate that you pay your fee. And you will. (Trust me, it is better to pay £100 now and become consistent than to keep those £100 in your pocket and never achieve your goal. Your goal is worth much more than that.)

Accountability partners must have certain characteristics. Firstly, they need to be very strict with you. You do not want someone who will pity you when you do not manage to do what you agreed, but instead someone who will push you to give your best. Secondly, if they are your accountability partner, ideally you should not be theirs. Why? Because in the event that you have a lazy day and they have a lazy day too, you may both be tempted to turn a blind eye rather than push each other. It is better if there is a one-way check; it will be a more objective partnership.

Words: 309   Time (in seconds): _____

Killer no. 5: Expecting Too Much—the Law of Input–Output

{Easy Peasy layer}

Optimism can be useful in many moments of your life, but not when you are working towards a goal. The problem is that we tend to set goals when we are motivated. Although a wonderful thing in itself, this in turn leads us to overestimate what we can actually do: not just in terms of goals, but in terms of tangible daily actions. And nothing kills your motivation more than not achieving something at a moment in which your motivation is high. The reason behind this is simple; 'If you are not able to stick to your plan even on a good day, imagine what a bad one would look like!' is exactly what your mind will tell you.

As a result, we need to do something to prevent this from happening. And while all the measures you have read about in the previous paragraphs will help you immensely, adding the Law of Input–Output will add a greater value. It will make it simpler to complete your daily tasks, so that your motivation can increase day by day. Your motivation is fuelled by your successes—so let's create a lot of successes to grow your motivation and achieve your goal.

First, set your medium-term goal (two weeks is usually a great initial term as it is long enough for you to have time to achieve something remarkable, but not long enough for you to lose track of your target).

Second, divide the two-week goal by ten to select the actions you need to achieve daily (going by five days per week, so you can have a cushion in case something goes wrong). For example, if you want to learn five hundred Spanish words in two weeks, your daily goal will be to memorise fifty words. If you want to read a 1,000-page book, your daily goal will be to read one hundred pages. If you want to prepare for an exam on ten videos and five articles, your daily goal will be to watch one video and read half an article. And so on.

Third, assess how long it will take you to reach the daily goal, to make sure your goal is properly calibrated. If you are able to put in the required time each day, move on to the next step; if not, re-adjust the goal so that it becomes feasible.

Fourth, once you see that the daily task is doable, set your daily goal to make it so that every day you will need to reach that goal or put in that time. For example, if you know that studying fifty words takes you thirty-five minutes, every day your goal will be to either learn fifty words or to study for fifty minutes (it is better to be generous with your time in case you have a bad day); and if you know that reading one hundred pages takes you fifty minutes, every day your goal will be to either read one hundred pages or read for seventy minutes.

When you reach either of the two goals, you can consider your daily task complete.

This process, in all its apparent simplicity, will prove an almighty weapon for success.

There are two kinds of people in the world: those who work best when they are focused on the goal they need to achieve (output), and those who work best when they are focused on the actions they need to take (input). To be precise, all people may work better with one or the other according to the goal that they set for themselves and the mood they are in. This strategy will help you to keep both input and output in mind, which is a release for your conscience and a boost for your motivation.

As soon as you hit your input or your output, you are done for the day. Anything else you do, it is an extra, not a due.

I'll give a quick example of how this can be a lifesaver for your motivation even in an extreme case.

Let's say that after a couple of days you realise your input had not been calculated correctly, which is to say that you need more time to achieve your daily goal than you had originally anticipated. If you had only set a daily output goal (like most people do), you would feel day after day that you are failing, that you are always behind. Every new morning, you would be heading off uphill, needing to chase a result that day after day seems less achievable and more distant.

However, since you have set input and output goals, what happens? On the first day you notice that you may have been over-optimistic in selecting how much time (input) you would take to achieve your result (output), but you complete your input goal and so your conscience is ok. On the second day, you start again and want to check whether day one was just a bad day or if actually you are very unlikely to achieve the result (output goal) in the established time (input goal). If you realise you need more time per day, you can evaluate whether you have that time at your disposal or not, and whether the two-day cushions you have will be enough to repair the situation. If not, you will adjust the goal so that it is achievable, and the catharsis that comes from having been consistent to your plan will be a great way to face the unexpected challenge with the best mood.

I have never seen people achieve as many goals and with as much consistency as after I invented this technique. Use it wisely.

Words: 954   *Time (in seconds):* _____

Killer no. 6: Looking Back—the Law of the Blank Page

{No effort layer}

There is something else that can seriously sabotage your results and that only you have the power to change: your internal dialogue. Especially when it constantly looks back instead of forward.

In your past you may have been a wonderful learner or you may have struggled with every possible subject.

It. Is. Not. Your. Fault.

You need to repeat these words until they are embedded in you.

Everyone who knows me knows how importantly I take the concept of responsibility. I believe that only by taking full responsibility for what happens to you do you have the power to change anything (we said *Genius by Choice*, didn't we?). However, you are not responsible for how you were taught to study. Maybe you found a teacher that really understood you and allowed you to discover your own way of learning things. Maybe—as unfortunately happens to most—your teacher had no idea that every student could be a 'genius' if taught properly; so they taught you the way they knew, but that way was not *your* way, and you always struggled. Maybe you even started believing that studying was not for you, or that you were not that clever or that smart.

Well, I am here to tell you that the only reason why you did not succeed was because no one taught you in the right way. At Genius in 21 Days our Mentors spend hours understanding the cognitive profile of each client: analysing it and making a plan. The goal is not only to help you achieve your most imminent goals but to also ensure you become autonomous and independent. Shaping your own method according to your unique characteristics is the only way to make sure that you finally learn the best way for you.

The first thing you need to keep in mind, however, is that as long as you believe the voice that tells you that *you* are the problem, you won't bring out your full potential. Let me tell you one more time. You are not the problem. The problem was the wrong teaching method.

Now you finally have the possibility to create a method that works for you, because it comes from years and years of experience across thousands of clients. In a book it is impossible to mentor you one-to-one, but at the same time all the techniques I have selected are designed to help you regardless of your cognitive profile.

In front of you right now is a blank page, where all that matters is your willingness to learn. Every time you catch yourself thinking about your past results, ask yourself to look at this blank page instead, and to start picturing what you want to write on it. Ask yourself how you can have more fun while doing it, how you can enjoy it more.

You are about to take learning into your own hands, and it will be an amazing experience.

Words: 492 *Time (in seconds): _____*

CHAPTER FOUR

Time

[Bed is fine]

Have you ever had one of those days in which you do a lot of things, but when you get home you have the feeling of dissatisfaction and emptiness, as if you had not really accomplished anything?

At times, you may invest all your energy in what needs to be done. However, since there are so many things that require your attention, you do not always know where to start. What people therefore tend to do is to begin either with what they love doing the most, or with what they would rather not do at all (the 'eat the frog' concept). But come the end of the day they still do not feel confident in calling their day 'productive'.

This worsens when you also have to manage other people's work besides your own: the situation becomes even more complicated.

How can you prioritise tasks and keep a clear vision of the big picture while also being aware of all the little details, avoiding distraction and keeping your eye on the ball, even when tired or bored?

Whether you are studying for an exam or working on a project, this applies to both. Every time you have to take care of a small or big project, if you want to carry it out at your best, you need to raise the level of your efficiency.

In this part you are going to understand what mistakes to avoid (and how), and you will learn the DESIRE technique, which will help you become extremely efficient in your organisation while keeping your precious freedom. Finally, you will learn some strategies on how to stick to the plan because a plan can be wonderful on paper, but no plan is wonderful if it does not get done.

Words: 293   Time (in seconds): _____

Main mistakes
{No effort layer}

The two prisons we build

I know many people who would never give up on their freedom by following a plan. I also know some who do stick to their plan, but do so with a sense of imprisonment, as if they had no other choice. This happens because, if you think about it, what are the first real schedules you had to stick to? For most, it was your school schedule: with certain subjects taught at certain times, certain homework for certain days, and so on. From being a child who was free to play at any time, you turned into a child who had to be organised. And you lost your freedom.

The reality is that freedom and (proper) planning are related, yes, but in the opposite way. When you do not plan effectively what happens? Unforeseen things come up, and you need to react to them. A deadline approaches, you are behind, and you lose your freedom to do anything else because you need to catch up. Others arrange meetings for you instead of you choosing. You receive emails and messages and feel you must respond, dropping anything else you were doing. The outside world dictates your time. You become a slave to external circumstances. You are in jail. Now, I am not saying that you should organise everything, because that is another prison you can build around yourself. I know people who plan every single second of their life, and this does not leave room for surprises, intuition, creativity, flow, fun. So if you are one of those people who plan everything in detail, you are going to find something interesting here too: to make your life lighter, more enjoyable and more flexible, without giving up on the results that your organisation helps you achieve.

The key, as usual, is in the balance.

Planning based on dreams rather than facts

One huge mistake people make is that they dream a lot (which is good in itself), but they do not undertake a reality check to ensure their dream can be realised. When you are motivated, you tend to set goals that do not take into account the actual effort you need to put in in order to achieve them. I am not saying that none of the goals you set for yourself when you are motivated will be achieved; but you should take particular care in ensuring that the steps you must take to fulfil your dream are not only feasible but also sustainable over time.

For this reason, in the planning strategy that we will explore, there will be some reality checks and adjustments that you will need to make to your plan. It is important to keep aiming high, but if you aim high and you fail this could create a very bad bug in your system, which will sabotage your next goals unless you take measures to prevent it.

One important principle you will need to follow is that you cannot improve what you do not measure. You will notice that I will constantly ask you to measure things: from how long it takes you to complete a certain task, to how many pages you can study in a certain time, to how many words you can read in a minute, and so on. The stopwatch on your phone will become a great friend of yours.

At the beginning, for those of you who prefer 'going with the flow', it may feel weird to measure anything. My suggestion is this: try. I am not going to ask you to measure *everything*, but there is *something* that, when measured, can take you to excellence. Trying is harmless.

Being reactive rather than proactive

One of the poisons to your time management is that nowadays it is extremely easy to be reached by others. Be it an email, a phone call, a text, a message on social media, we are bombarded with notifications.

The state of mind you need to get into is what I call the Proactive MO (*modus operandi*). People with a Reactive MO tend to react to anything that happens to them. If they receive a text, they answer as soon as possible, interrupting anything they are doing. If someone approaches their desk, they engage in any conversation and usually even say yes to any request, dropping whatever they are dealing with and readjusting their whole schedule.

When you acquire a Proactive MO, your life changes immediately. I experienced this myself. There was a moment in which I was supervising so many projects, training so many people and taking care of so many different areas of my business that I felt I was becoming overwhelmed. I had always considered myself to be pretty organised, but I was not able to keep up anymore, and I thought that maybe I had taken on too much this time.

I was ready to drop some of these projects and postpone them to a later date, when I had a simple (but life-changing, at least for these projects) intuition. The reason I was struggling to keep up with everything was because I thought I was organised, but I actually was not. Or better, I was, but I was making a huge mistake: I still felt compelled to respond to most messages and calls promptly, and this was taking energy, focus and momentum away from everything else. The result was that I would respond to those texts, but I would do so in a rush, not always giving them my full focus because I had other things to juggle; and those other things would lose momentum, meaning I had to restore it every time.

I changed my MO, and I informed my clients and collaborators about it. I said: 'From now on, I will allocate some time every day (or every two, three—this changes according to the activity) to check on you and respond to any request. So, if I do not answer straight away, I am not ignoring you, do not worry. If you need something urgently, please write "URGENT" on top of the text, so I can tackle it as soon as I am out of meetings.' And guess what their reaction was? They loved it! They felt appreciated because I allocated some time in my routine specifically to them, and I felt free to focus on what I had to do rather than reacting to everything that was around.

Moving from a Reactive MO to a Proactive MO liberated me.

Having a break when you are exhausted

When you have a lot of things to do, you will be tempted to do as much as possible in a row, as if taking a break was a guilty pleasure you could not afford. The reality is that we have heard way too many times that 'first you work, then you can play'. On one side it makes sense, but on the other this attitude creates a lot of problems. When your task lasts up to a couple of hours or so, 'first work, then play' works very well. When you have a long task ahead of you, it creates a lot of damage.

The reason is that our body and mind, in order to function effectively, need some rest. You cannot stretch them forever. You need to give them a moment in which to switch off. Imagine you want to breathe, and you start breathing in. Then you keep breathing in. And you breathe in more. And more. Come a certain point, your body will not be able to, because it needs to make space for the new air to come in, and it does so by breathing out.

The same applies to your mind when you want to learn something. If you keep putting things in, and in, and in, and in, without resting and recharging, you will explode (metaphorically). You need to give yourself a break. When we come to talk about the strategies to organise your actual study time you will see how long breaks should be in order to be effective (Chapter Five—Cycles).

Not managing the unexpected

Buffers are another important aspect to keep in mind when planning. I see plans of 'motivated' people that do not include a single free moment, sometimes not even for lunch! It is very unrealistic to never have some downtime, so make sure you include some empty hours in your plan. The other reason why these empty hours are necessary is because unforeseen circumstances can come up. And will. A task may take longer than you expected; someone may need some urgent help; you may have more emails than usual to answer; and so on. It is important to incorporate some buffers to help you manage the unforeseeable, so that—just in case—you can have some extra time to take care of whatever needs your attention. If, instead, you do succeed in doing everything you had to do in the time allocated, you can use your buffer to either rest and relax or to do something out of your Ready-To-Do Map.

Planning day by day

When people ask me to help them with their time management, the first thing I do is to understand what they are currently doing to organise their time. Most people organise their life day by day, deciding what they want to accomplish by the end of the day and making a list out of it. Although this is better than not having a clue about what you want to get done, there is a big risk that comes with this strategy unless you are very experienced: very often, the items on your daily to do list are the things that you must do.

You may re-read that last sentence to understand what is wrong with it. After all, should you not do what you must do?

Yes, you should, but you should not forget about what you want to do, which is all those actions that will take you closer to your longer-term goal. Planning day by day can be done only if you are able to keep your eyes on the big picture. A much better approach is to set your goals for one year, and then break them down to six months, a quarter, a month.

After you have identified what you want to accomplish by the end of the month in each area of your life, you can start planning week by week. A week is a great unit of measurement, as it is a long enough time for you to include what you need in order to reach your longer-term goals, while at the same time being short enough for you to be in control of your time.

Words: 1,800 *Time (in seconds):* _____

Planning
{Easy Peasy layer}

Very often people think the difficulty in sticking to the plan is due to their lack of discipline or laziness. The reality is that more than half of the work required to stick to the plan is done while planning; and, if you plan effectively, you will save a lot of time and effort when it comes to sticking to it, and doing so will be almost child's play.

The DESIRE Technique

Over the years, I have developed a six-step process (the DESIRE Technique), which is the juice of years spent adjusting strategies to ensure they would please every kind of person. The reality is that your organisation style—as with every kind of skill—is also extremely affected by your cognitive styles. The DESIRE Technique does its best to take these into consideration, making it simple for you to plan effectively regardless of your style.

When you apply the DESIRE Technique, make sure to take the measures we discussed in the previous chapter to avoid the mistakes you may have made in the past. Do not create either of the two prisons; get into the habit of measuring, so that you can plan based on facts; find your strategies to adopt a proactive MO instead of a reactive one; plan your breaks in advance; keep some buffers to manage unforeseen situations; and plan your week, keeping an eye on your longer-term goals.

Now it is time to explore the DESIRE Technique.

To apply it effectively, you will need a pen, some colours (optional, but I find them very helpful) and two sheets of paper. An alternative is to use a sheet of paper and a weekly planner, but the sheet of paper instead of the planner also works very well (and at times even better).

D for Decide

The first step is to Decide what you want to get done by the end of the week. Do not give yourself any limit, just honestly write down all the things you would like to get done in a week. In this phase, do not worry about what is actually achievable or not, as you do not yet have enough elements to judge it. For now, allow yourself to dream. You will have time to ground yourself later.

The best tool you can use is a Mind Map (Chapter Thirteen), as it will help you form a global vision of all the things you want to do and will allow you to easily divide them into categories. If you are not familiar with Mind Maps yet, what you can do for now is use a list; though try as much as possible to split the goals and activities into categories, as it will help your mental organisation.

In this phase, include everything that comes to mind: what you are dragging from the previous week; what you want to study; emails you need to reply to; calls you need to make; how many times you want to exercise or meditate; the actions you need to take to achieve some specific goals; and so on.

E for Estimate

Here comes a phase that a lot of people do not focus their attention on, but which will have a huge impact on how able you will be to stick to your plan. What you will need to estimate, as accurately as possible, is how long each task will take.

At the beginning, if you have never paid much attention to how long it takes you to complete certain tasks, this phase may be a bit hard for you. Do not worry: once you do it a few times, you will notice stunning improvements. For now, make sure that when in doubt you overestimate rather than underestimate the amount of time required. Remember that for longer activities you will need to include breaks in the time you write down.

Acing this phase will make you a champion of productivity and freedom, so practise with it until you can accurately estimate the time of each task.

While estimating the times, what may happen is that you realise some of those tasks on your map/list should be split into different sub-tasks. As you become more of an expert, this will no longer happen; but for now whenever it does happen split them up, so that you can time each part properly.

At the end of this process, add up all the times to get to the total and write it down on your map/list.

S for Scheduled

For this phase, all you need to do is to take the second sheet of paper or your weekly planner and write down only the commitments (appointments and activities) that are already scheduled. If you are in the habit of noting them in your diary, it will be a very quick phase as you will just copy them down. If you are not in that habit yet, create it as soon as possible: it will relieve your mind from keeping a mental track of everything.

I know some people love using the calendar on their phone to write in all their meetings, and I do too. However, when planning your week it is easier to do this on paper rather than on your phone, given that having more space in front of you will allow you to have a better global vision.

I for Investigate

This is the phase in which you turn your dreams into goals. To do it, you need to investigate whether there is enough time in your diary to fit all the tasks you wrote on your map/list. If, initially, this had been impossible to determine, now that you have estimated the times and written down what you have already scheduled it simply becomes a matter of calculating.

When counting your available hours, I can never stress enough how fundamental it is for you to keep buffers. During the day there will be unexpected things coming up; there will be interruptions; there will be emergencies to take care of. Having buffers is what will save you, so include them. A full schedule is a wrong schedule.

If you are afraid that those buffer times may go to waste if on that day there are no emergencies, do not worry: we are going to see how to make good use of them.

R for Revisit

After Investigating, you may find yourself in one of three situations. From the least to the most frequent, these are as follows: the available hours that you have on your schedule are exactly those you need to complete the tasks on your map/list (the rarest); you have much more time than you need to complete you tasks (rare); you do not have enough time to complete all the tasks on your map/list (frequent).

According to what situation you find yourself in, you will revisit your map/list and adjust it.

In the rare instance where you have much more time than your tasks require, go back to your map and add some more goals that you can achieve that week.

In the far more frequent case in which you find yourself having more items on your map than are possibly achievable, there are some measures you can take when revisiting it.

Prioritise

First of all, you need to prioritise your tasks; selecting the ones that are more urgent, but not overlooking those that may be due later yet require more time. You may decide to get some urgent stuff done, while also starting on some longer-term tasks that you will otherwise not be able to finish in time.

Balance

This is paramount. When you prioritise your tasks, do not forget to include those activities that may not be urgent, but which are important. When time is tight, there are people who choose to cut down on those activities that do not have a deadline—such as exercising, studying, planning, taking care of their health, and so on. Do not make this big mistake. It may look like a winning choice in the short term, but it will create irreparable damage in the future.

E for Ending

After you have finalised your choice of tasks, insert them into your plan so that you can finish it.

What I like doing is to colour the edges of the blocks of time: not according to the specific activity but to the category—personal health and development, business growth, marketing, admin, and so on. This allows me to have a quick understanding of how balanced I have been in my plan. There may be weeks in which one area requires way more time than others, and that is fine, but it is important to monitor this: at times the areas you are spending more time on are not necessarily the ones that can help you achieve the goals you have.

Space for ticks
As the days go by, you will tick off the activities that you complete. (You might do so by colouring them, or by writing a tick or a dot—the method you choose does not matter.) Doing so will give you an understanding of how much you actually achieve compared to what you plan, and will allow you to analyse your results with a non-judgmental, scientific mind that can see what went great and where improvement is needed.

PRO HACK

If you are someone who particularly struggles with discipline, I have another tip for you. When writing down your activities on your plan, split each day into two columns. In the left column you will write your plan, while in the right one you will write hour by hour what you actually do. The goal is for them to match. If they often do not, use your scientific mind to analyse what activities you are not completing and why, so that you can take measures for the following week. However, if you follow the DESIRE Technique step by step and the techniques that will be described when talking about sticking to the plan, this will happen very rarely, as you will already have avoided most of the pitfalls people will encounter. This will help you analyse with even more accuracy what is causing your lack of discipline, and will give you that visual aid that, for many, makes the difference in raising their awareness.

Ready-To-Do Map

I promised that you would not waste your buffer times, and I always keep my promises. This is the purpose of the Ready-To-Do Map.

One of the advantages of having a plan is that, when moving from one activity to another, you do not need to waste time thinking about what to do, as you have already done it.

If it is true that your buffers look empty, they are not. They are jokers for you. When you need to use them to deal with emergencies or urgent situations, they are there for you. However, when everything is going smoothly, they will be the moments in which you can take care of other tasks.

To prevent you from wasting precious time thinking about what to do, you will have a Ready-To-Do Map, where you will include those things that need to be done but do not have a deadline or a specific time in which to be taken care. Keep it with you always, as there may be times in which you find yourself waiting for someone, or finishing something earlier, and it is great if—instead of wasting that time—you can put it to good use.

Remember: buffers are not breaks. Breaks should already be included in your plan. Buffers are joker times that will adapt to what you need the most in that moment.

Words: 1,966   *Time (in seconds): _____*

Sticking to the plan
{No effort layer}

Here we come to one of the most sought-after skills. Whenever I run a Q&A session, the following question is always present, and is usually one of the first to come up: 'How can I be more disciplined?'

It has probably happened to everyone. You have some or other goal, you are motivated, you create a plan. The time comes to put your plan into action, and you just cannot seem to be able to do it. You postpone, you do not put all the focus you should, things start dragging out, and you cannot complete what looked like a perfect plan.

There are four main reasons why you can find it hard to stick to your plan, and almost none of them has to do with sticking to the plan!

Reason One: Wrong Planning

As we discussed a few pages ago (in Chapter Four), most of the difficulty in sticking to the plan comes from planning poorly. Make sure you apply the DESIRE Technique, and most of your problems will disappear.

Reason Two: Laziness

The second reason why sticking to the plan may be hard has to do with your supposed laziness. Even though I believe that every human being has a lazy side, I do not believe that laziness has anything to do with not sticking to your plan. It is a matter of remembering why you want to do it, and the best way to defeat your 'laziness' is by applying the seven Laws to the killers of motivation (Chapter Three—Motivation).

Reason Three: Wrong Estimation

A lot of people who are working on their time management abilities stumble on this point. This is completely normal, as it takes practice to get it right if you are not used to it. The second step of the DESIRE Technique is to Estimate how long each task will take. If for some of them this turns out to be very simple (appointments and tasks that you have done several times), for other activities it may be challenging to allocate the appropriate amount of time.

Even as you improve your estimating skills, there will be days in which a task will just take longer than you expected. Not everything is predictable.

When you get to the end of the time allocated for a specific task and you have not finished it, what do you usually do? I know that many people keep going with that task and postpone everything else. The problem with this is that you will create a growing pile of other, uncompleted tasks, and this will lead to the collapse of your plan.

Of course, be flexible: there will be times in which the task that you have not managed to complete is extremely urgent, and in that case you will go on with it. But this should be the exception, rather than the norm.

As a general rule, if your time slot for that task ends, you will move on to the next task, which is the same thing that you would naturally do if the following task was a meeting with someone. You would stop what you are doing and pick it back up later, so you can take your meeting. You need to start approaching each task as a meeting between you and your task, or you and yourself. You would not skip a meeting just because you have not completed something, would you?

In your plan, if you have followed the DESIRE Technique, you will have included some buffers: those are the moments in which you will pick up the incomplete task in order to get it done.

There is one more step you need to take. With the eye of a scientist, make sure you understand why you had underestimated the time that a certain activity would require. Only when you get into the habit of analysing what works and what does not will you know yourself and create your success recipe.

Reason Four: Interruptions

Another reason why you may not be able to stick to the plan is due to interruptions. There are two kinds of interruptions: internal and external.

Internal interruptions are also known as distractions. They are those moments in which you start wondering about what you should eat at lunch, how to change the world, or why the author of the book keeps using the word *tantalising*. You get the gist.

To reduce internal distractions, the first step is to read Create Your Momentum (Chapter Three), especially focusing on the paragraphs Stop Internal Distractions and Focus. Study. Pause. Repeat.

External interruptions, on the other hand, do not depend solely on you, but can still be classified and dealt with.

The first level is made up of those interruptions that can easily be avoided, namely notifications. Removing your notifications while you are working on a task, although an obvious action to take, is not that frequently employed. There are some notifications that we just feel we should not remove, because 'You never know, it could be urgent.'

Yes, it may be urgent. But when you are in a meeting with someone, do you keep checking your notifications? I hope not. The world will (usually) not stop spinning if for one hour you do not check your phone. But the productivity of that hour will receive a boost. Being constantly interrupted by notifications breaks your momentum, and you will need to use much more energy to get back into the zone again. If you work in an environment where you know that notifications need to be dealt with more often than every hour, have a moment every half hour in which you take care of them. Regardless of checking them every thirty, sixty or ninety minutes, it will be a relief for your mind to be finally able to focus on one task at a time.

The second level of external interruptions concerns urgent requests from other people. It is not uncommon for a colleague or your boss to ask you to get something done. (For students, the same applies to classmates or parents asking for help with school or chores). As usual, be flexible, but make sure you realise that always saying yes will push you away from your goals. It requires a lot of assertiveness to say no when someone is asking for help. Everyone who knows me knows that I love helping whenever I can, and so this was a point on which I had to work hard. Helping is wonderful: it makes you feel fulfilled and it benefits someone else; but there is a difference between helping when you can and helping when you cannot.

I approach this by first establishing when their deadline in; how long it will take me to help this person; and whether I am the only one who can help, or if there is someone else who is as able and more available than me.

Then I check my daily buffers. If they are still free, I will ask the person who is looking for my help if it is fine for me to deal with the request at the specific time of my buffer. If it is more urgent than that, I see if I can swap my buffer with my current activity, and in that case I have not removed anything from my plan.

There are times in which you are unable help out, and you must learn how to say 'I am sorry, I cannot do it today. Is it fine if I do it tomorrow or can I suggest someone else you could ask?' It is more mature to say no than to say yes at the expense of either your goals or theirs.

The third level of external interruptions is what I classify as 'emergencies': those urgent things that require your immediate attention. In this case, take care of the emergency and make sure you revisit your plan to make up for the time you lost.

PRO HACK Percentages

People ask me at what point they can consider their sticking to the plan 'good enough'. A lot depends on what you do and what margin of unpredictability your job has. If you work in a team and your ability to stick to the plan does not depend entirely on you, reaching eighty per cent of your weekly plan can be considered a good result. If you are the only person responsible for what you choose to do each day, ninety per cent will be the threshold. Always aim for perfection, but remember that perfection is hardly sustainable, especially if you aim to become better and better and to raise the bar. Be flexible, but be honest with yourself. Could you have done that thing that you did not? What happened? How can you prevent it next time? Your Genius Journal will help you to keep track of these observations.

Words: 1,485 *Time (in seconds): _____*

Note to self: include some time to plan your strategy

This will be a short paragraph, but it will teach you one of those things that most people do not do, yet which after hearing about just makes sense—something that can make the difference between being lost at sea and having a lighthouse in front of you to show you the way.

When people have a book to study, a big presentation to prepare, an exam to pass or any other big learning task in front of them, what the majority tend to do is to dive into reading the texts and studying them. What really makes a difference, though, is investing some time beforehand to gather all the information required if you are to succeed, especially when your task will involve some evaluation from someone else.

So, the first phase—which you should never miss—needs to be spent researching what it is that you need in order to succeed.

Let's say you want to pass a qualification exam to enhance your career. I see many people who buy the material and dive into it, without first researching what is actually required to pass that exam. There are websites where you can find past exam papers, suggestions from people who have already passed that exam, advice from the institution that delivers it, or formal descriptions of what is actually required. Building this knowledge in your mind may require you to invest a few minutes or a few days, according to how big the task ahead of you is, but it will save you much more time than you invest throughout the learning process and will increase your chances of succeeding.

The same applies when you want to prepare for a presentation. What is the purpose of this presentation? This will allow you to choose what to say and what to keep in mind so that the audience is not overwhelmed.

Could you imagine a General going to battle without preparing? Sure, he would act faster, but are you sure he would be proud of the result?

Words: 338   *Time (in seconds):* _____

CHAPTER FIVE

Create Your Momentum

[Bed is fine]

Your Study Sanctuary
{No effort layer}

The environment around you will have a huge impact on your ability to focus, so let's see how you can make yours better.

Strategy one: go back in time

All of us are different, and this applies to choosing the perfect environment in which study. The best thing you could do is to think back to a time in which you really felt focused and concentrated (if it ever happened!). Where were you? In your room? In a library? In a park? At school? In a café? There is no right answer.

Go back to that moment and analyse what sounds defined that environment. Nature sounds? Light music? Silence?

Analyse what objects were present in that environment. Were there many of them? Were they tidy or messy? What were the main colours?

Reproduce every aspect that you can in your Study Sanctuary. If you were in a park and you now need to study indoors, make sure you have a plant in sight, and find a soundtrack with sounds from nature to take you back to that moment and that concentration state.

Strategy two: experiment

At times you may not remember one specific occasion in which you were very focused, or you may not remember the details of that environment. At times you would like to find more spaces in which you can experience extreme concentration. In such cases, you must start experimenting. Here you will find some guidelines that will help you create your personal Study Sanctuary.

Music: yes or no

One of the most common questions people ask me about keeping their focus high while learning is whether or not it is good to keep some background music on.

As always, you will need to be flexible and get to know yourself. Music can be a great way to isolate oneself from external distractions, especially if one of your cognitive styles is Field Dependent. However, the wrong kind of music could become a distraction in itself.

Usually, people who are prone to distraction will work well either with noise-cancelling earphones or with music that is without lyrics. Classical music or sounds of nature will help.

On the other hand, I also know people who thrive when listening to techno and metal music—something that others would find extremely distracting—because the strong beats and fast pace help keep their rhythm and energy high.

If your Natural Intelligence is very strong, sounds of nature will be your best choice, as they will take you back to an environment in which your connection and focus are higher. Try, try, try.

Light

Keeping your lighting right will be important for your focus. You do not want to keep straining your eyes to be able to read because it is too dark, just as you do not wish to be annoyed by excessive light. Whenever possible, rely on natural light more than lightbulbs, but when natural light is not enough, brightness is better than darkness.

Posture

Posture is an interesting topic, as theories about this have evolved over the years.

I will tell you what the proper posture should look like and why, but keep in mind that it will not always be the best option for everyone, and we will see how you can adjust it according to your preference.

A perfect reading posture will see you sitting down at a desk with your back straight, your book in front of you, your feet placed on the floor. The chair should not be too soft as its main role will be to support your back while you read.

Imagine you have a straw and you bend it: liquid and air will struggle to come through. A similar thing happens to our body. When you bend your neck in order to read, not only will you feel uncomfortable if you keep that posture for a while, but you will also be preventing oxygen from flowing correctly, which will lead to distraction and lack of lucidity. This is why you should sit straight, and, when you bend, you should bend from the waist rather than from the neck. In the part about Strategic Reading, we will get to know a tool that can help immensely with this.

However, if it is true that perfect posture gives incredible advantages, not everyone will find it the best option for them all the time. The reason lies in the fact that there are multiple learning styles. For some kinds of learners, changing posture is more important than keeping a perfect one, especially when they need to study or work for a lot of hours. For example, I like changing my position and my posture frequently. At times you will find me at my desk, at times on the floor, at a high table or a low one, on the couch or in bed. Textbooks do not advise you to do it, but I started becoming much more productive when I allowed myself to change rather than forcing myself to sit properly the whole time. Once I explored the concept of learning styles and multiple intelligences deeper, I understood why and I no longer felt that I was 'breaking the rules'; I was just following my natural disposition.

As usual, be an explorer, so that you can get to know yourself better and find your own way.

Words: 891 *Time (in seconds):* _____

Your Success Kit
{Easy Peasy layer}

Another important aspect to include when preparing your Sanctuary is the objects you may need throughout the session (your Success Kit). There is nothing worse than entering the zone and having to break the flow because you need to get a pen.

So, what is in the Success Kit that will help you achieve your goals?

- texts you need to learn from
- access to a browser
- pen
- paper
- colours
- chopstick
- bookstand (optional)
- stopwatch
- timer
- water
- snacks (if you know you like munching while learning)

The use of some objects in your Success Kit may as of yet be unclear, but as we go ahead you will find out how to use all of these eleven items: access to a browser (Chapter Eleven—Decoding and Understanding); pen, colours and paper—you can substitute them with a tablet if you have one (next paragraph and Chapter Thirteen—passage on Mind Maps); chopstick and bookstand (Chapter Six—passage on Strategic Reading); stopwatch (Chapter Four—Time); timer (Chapter Five—paragraph on Pomodoro)

Your Genius Journal

Your Genius Journal is a tool that will help you in the process of increasing your skills and unleashing your intrinsic motivation more and more.

What you need to do is have a journal that you keep next to you any time you study or learn anything. At the end of each learning session, you will invest two minutes (maximum) to record the following things: what time of day it is, what new strategies you have experimented with (if any), your general condition (tired, excited, long day), how much you learned, and why.

By going to geniusbychoice.co.uk/gift you will be able to download the blueprints for the Genius Journal and much more.

Your goal is to take note so that you can use your scientific mind to analyse what works best for you, to track your progress, to check what to improve in the following session, and so on.

It is a tool that does not require anything other than two minutes after your learning session, but which shall make a huge difference in the self-awareness you will develop about how you learn.

Words: 336   *Time (in seconds):* _____

Stop Internal Distractions
{Easy Peasy layer}

Internal distractions are all the thoughts that enter your mind while you are (supposedly) focused on a task. These include other things to do, things you should have done or said, ideas to change the world, trains of thoughts about the most unexpected of subjects, deeper dives you would like to take on the topic you are reading, and so on.

To fix this inevitable consequence of our mind's incessant activity, use a Distraction Sheet. What do I mean by this? Keep a white sheet of paper next to you during your session, and every time a thought comes to your mind to distract you, write it down on the sheet.

This practice is extremely helpful for a couple of reasons. First, if you do not write these thoughts down, part of your mind will feel obliged to keep thinking about them to prevent you forgetting. You can imagine how distracting that will be. A second reason is that the other logical option would be to take care of those thoughts by dropping what you are doing. It seems silly, but it is more often than not what actually happens. The problem with this is that, once the momentum is broken, you need to create it again, and so when you go back to doing what you interrupted, you will find yourself wasting significant time re-entering the zone. By noting down your distracting thought on a sheet of paper, the benefit will be double: for one the time to note down one word is so short that your momentum will not be broken; and secondly, by writing the thought on paper, your mind will not need to worry that you may forget it, freeing it to focus on your task once more.

When you reach your break, you will then be able to take care of everything, and you will have achieved much more in your session than you would have by keeping your thoughts active in the back of your mind while attempting to focus on your task.

Words: 340   Time (in seconds): _____

Focus. Study. Pause. Repeat.
{Easy Peasy layer}

Creating momentum is not just a matter of removing distractions, but instead entering a state of flow where you can be extremely productive. To achieve this state, you will need to create a rhythm that is sustainable and that allows your mind to maintain a high focus over a period of time.

Attention spans vary across every human being, so we are going to discuss what factors you need to keep in mind and a strategy for you to adapt accordingly.

What affects your attention

'Oh, this technology!' I hear it all the time: since the advent of social media, people's attention spans have decreased immensely.

Although it is true that social media is not renowned for helping increase your attention span, the causes of your distraction are not purely attributable to it.

Circadian Rhythms and Chronotype

Across the twenty-four hours of a day, your level of attention and cognitive functions will greatly vary. Are you a night owl or a lark? Identifying your chronotype and understanding your circadian rhythms will help you organise your day in a way that suits your body and your natural cycles. It will help you to decide when to exercise and when to study or work, and also to choose what is the best time to tackle more challenging tasks.

The first way to understand it is to keep track of your performance in your Genius Journal, where you will note down any big change in your level of attention. If you notice that exercising in the morning activates your energy, wonderful; but you may also notice that certain kinds of exercise leave you exhausted afterwards, and so you may want to leave them for the end of your day. Experimenting is always the key to awareness.

Learning Styles

We analyse many Learning Styles at Genius in 21 Days. Of these, there is one that (among other aspects) affects your ability to focus and, as a consequence, the strategies you should choose. It is called Field Dependence vs Field Independence. If you are a Field Dependent learner, you will tend to focus your attention on the environment as a whole, which may lead you to becoming distracted very easily. Not having a clear structure to follow, or working on your own rather than in a team, will also increase the likelihood of distraction.

If you are a Field Independent learner, your source of distraction may be very different, and you will need to adapt your strategies to enhance the strengths of your style while preventing the risks that come with it.

Eat, Sleep, Exercise.

Needless to say, a good night's sleep will increase your attention span, whereas being deprived of sleep for even one night will have a negative impact. Minding the food that you eat and the exercise you do will help you increase your ability to concentrate, as will meditation.

Difficulty and Emotions

The difficulty level of what you are reading and the emotional state that you are in will also affect your attention, so make sure that you read the chapter on Motivation very carefully (Chapter Three) and that you apply everything in this book to change your perception of how hard the topic in front of you is.

How to increase your focus

Taking everything into account will help you to be more focused on the task in front of you. I will never get tired of repeating how important it is that you get to know how you personally work.

Of the many concentration techniques you can apply, I want to suggest one that is extremely simple and effective. All you need to do is to sit comfortably, close your eyes and, one by one, imagine all the colours of the rainbow, from red to violet. For some people picturing a colour in their mind will come very naturally, while others may find it more beneficial to imagine an object (or more objects) that represents that colour. There is no right or wrong way, as long as you think about the colour. So, you will start with red, then you will move to orange, yellow, green, blue, indigo and violet. Allow yourself to linger on each colour for a few seconds before moving on to the next. Come the end, you will notice that your body and mind are much calmer than beforehand, and ahead of opening your eyes you may also want to try to state an intention for that session, to allow your mind to focus on the goal you have.

There are many other strategies that you can use, and no strategy is better than another, providing you can apply it simply and effectively.

Study Cycles

A lot of strategies have been created to help you keep your focus high for more hours in a day, without getting to the place at which you are so exhausted that you cannot think about anything anymore.

All these strategies have two things in common: they suggest avoiding multitasking to keep your full attention to one task, and they include breaks. We mentioned it already when we talked about the four mistakes people make when planning (Chapter Four). You must have breaks if you want to keep your momentum going. How often these breaks should happen will depend on all the elements I discussed a few pages back: your circadian rhythm, your learning styles, your level of well-being, your sleepiness, the difficulty of the task and the emotional state in which you are.

I recently read about a study carried out by Draugiem Group, in which they found that the most productive employees belonged to the ten per cent who would have a seventeen-minute break after fifty-two minutes of work.

The Pomodoro Technique suggests cycles of twenty-five minutes of work and five minutes of break to be repeated four times before a longer thirty-minute break.

Other studies suggest that your attention can span up to ninety minutes.

So what is the right answer?

Given that there are so many different elements that do not just depend on how you work, but also on what you are doing in that moment and your current well-being and alertness, I find the best strategy to be the following.

Start studying and set your timer to twenty-five minutes. This is the shortest time you should be able to keep your attention high for. (If you have ADHD, you may want to shorten that to fifteen minutes or even less).

When the timer goes off, assess how you are feeling. If you are in the zone and interrupting your work now would be painful for you—which may sound funny but happens more than you would imagine—reset the timer for another twenty-five minutes.

If, instead, you feel you could use a break, allow yourself five minutes in which you get up, drink some water, stretch and switch off. At that point, reset your timer for another twenty-five minutes.

If you have not had your break, then after a further twenty-five minutes the alarm will go off again and you will have worked or studied for fifty minutes straight, at which point it will be time to reassess.

Either you are rested and decide to do a third twenty-five-minute cycle, or you will appreciate a break and you will take a ten-minute pause.

After the third consecutive cycle, you will be seventy-five minutes in, so if you wanted to you could stretch it up to ninety minutes; though I would suggest that you have a fifteen-to-twenty minute break, before starting again from zero. It is always better to stop before you are exhausted. A break now is better than exhaustion later.

PRO HACK

When you apply the DESIRE Technique to plan your week (Chapter Four), make sure that when estimating times you always count one hour for every forty-five minutes of actual work. This will allow you to easily include the breaks without getting behind schedule.

Words: 1,340   *Time (in seconds):* _____

Inspiration Time from Our Genius Alumni

Initially, I was afraid the course wasn't worth the money but now I only regret not having taken it much sooner!

Every penny was totally worth it. I gained far more out of it than what we paid for it. I took the course twice, and each time I learnt something new (you can retake it within a year as many times as you want). After the course I had a Mentor who helped me deepen the techniques and especially how to tailor them for my own goals.

Within 2 weeks, I increased my reading speed from 172 words/minute to 473 and it has been growing since! Apart from that we learnt how to analyse texts and take notes in a far better way, so I was finding myself remembering 86% of what I have read without having memorised anything. I was reading the same amount in less time, and instead of finishing my essays just before midnight, I was shutting down the computer at 5pm, and could finally sleep much better. I felt much better.

After I was finished with my university modules, I said 'Hey, now that I have these advanced learning techniques, finally I can learn Italian', which I had been postponing for 10 years. On the first attempt in 18 days, I memorised 1012 words, then in 2 weeks' I did another 800. With another technique, I have learnt grammar and now I am on an elementary level only within weeks of putting time into learning a language.

And the best part is that while I could not study Italian for the last few months, I have not forgotten any of it. So, I was able to continue from where I left off, and still remember everything!

This course has given me so much more than just learning techniques. I have read 15 books of my choice this year so far (and it is only April!), while not one in the last few years before I took the course. I am really happy about this because it allowed me to put time into personal self-development, not just professional. For fun I have even learnt some sign language.

> What I realise is that with this tool set, there is no limit to what I can do if I put my mind to it. I feel finally that I have control over my life, that I can trust my abilities, and that I have freedom to choose how I spend my precious time.
>
> Nora Deme - Customer Experience Manager

PART II. READ

I recently read an article in which the author made it a point of destroying any hope that people had of reading faster, by providing facts that in his view were backed by science as to why our eyes cannot read more than a certain (small) amount of words per minute.

I agree with a lot of the points that he raised. Reading fast without understanding is not useful. If you want to go beyond certain thousands of words per minute you may give up on some comprehension (at times). Depending on the kind of text you are reading, you cannot expect to apply the same speed to every text. If you do not understand something you should not ignore it, rather you should go back to re-read it. All true.

But when he insisted on proving that it is not possible to read faster than about two hundred and eighty words per minute (or a bit more), I felt some tenderness. I know that speed-reading is not a magic wand, and I believe that too often people have valued speed over understanding, which makes no sense for the purpose of reading (as you will see in Chapter Seven). However, I have seen hundreds of people at Genius in 21 Days read four hundred, five hundred, even six hundred words per minute without giving up on their understanding, and that is why I feel the responsibility to teach you the tools that allow them to do so.

Is it just speed-reading techniques? No. This is why we call it Strategic Reading. Speed-reading techniques are helpful, and some tips are likely to make you twice as fast in a few minutes, but they are only one of the aspects that will help you read faster and better. Only by combining all the tools that you are learning in this book with a high awareness of your cognitive profile (which is different from anyone else's) will you achieve the kind of standard you may dream of.

Words: 338   *Time (in seconds):* _____

CHAPTER SIX

Assessment

[Desk is better]
{Easy Peasy layer}

Before we discuss anything about Strategic Reading I would like for you to assess your starting level, so that you can track your improvement later.

You will need to read the following text and answer the questions at the end of it. Before you start reading, prepare your stopwatch, as you will need to time how long it takes you to complete the task.

When you are finished, answer the questions without looking back at the text.

Learning—Extract from *The Brain: A User's Manual* by Marco Magrini

> Repetition over time is part of the learning game because that's how the memory mechanism works: neurons that fire together, says Hebb's Rule. It's the repeated use of the synapses that strengthens them. The crazy night spent studying before an exam can help us to pass the exam, but not to remember what has been studied long-term. Even the genius—albeit working less hard—must repeat the learning process again and again

over time if he or she wants to become a true genius. This is a way of saying that, no, there's no point in you looking for shortcuts either.

The learning machine is extraordinary. But it must be used. And used correctly.

We have talked about learning in generic terms but in actual fact it's a huge topic. Learning a foreign language, such as Polish or Spanish, 'lights up' many areas in the brain. Motor coordination, when, for example, learning to swim or skate, involves other regions of the brain. Playing the flute or the accordion involves a mix of the two, plus others. It's as though there were potentially a linguistic brain, a sports brain, a musical brain and so forth. There is room for all three in your skull, and for many more.

Since, during childhood and adolescence, neural development goes through so-called critical phases when certain kinds of learning are facilitated (languages, for instance, at preschool age), it's sensible to use the first period of your life to attend school and, at the same time, go to the swimming pool, take dance lessons and learn as much else as you can. However, this is where it comes down to families and, especially, governments, which manage public education.

There are as many education systems in the world as there are countries. Schools in Finland, which have been ranked first in the special classification devised by the World Economic Forum, are essentially different from those in Canada, Austria or Senegal. In general, however, the majority of school systems do not provide pupils with even basic information on that very brain they need in order to study (in an Italian secondary school textbook, we counted nine pages devoted to the brain and twelve to the digestive system), and do not even take discoveries in neuroscience into consideration.

To begin with, your standard strict teacher and rigid exam deadlines trigger the production of cortisol, the stress hormone. In the presence of fear signals, the most primitive functions of the brain end up opposing the more modern structures of the cortex, impairing how they work. In Finland, the first exam is not until the age of sixteen, the critical period appropriate for experiencing a little stress.

Naturally, even far away from Helsinki, there are wonderful teachers who do their jobs well, from kindergarten to university.

There are the ones who manage to make their teaching interesting if not actually fun, even if they are not aware of this being the only way to trigger the circulation of dopamine, which favours and strengthens synaptic connections.

They are the ones that step down from behind their raised desks and keep close contact with students, which is said to encourage the production of acetylcholine, the attention neuromodulator, in their student's brains.

They are the ones who bring new elements to the class (for example rearranging the classroom or using an original teaching solution), encouraging the spread of noradrenaline, which encourages attention and also, in the long run, attachment to studying.

And then, of course, if the pupils cross the line, they can always resort to a dose of adrenaline by raising their voices or threatening consequences. Still, they are the ones who do not brandish threats as a matter of habit, otherwise cortisol would ruin everything.

Now the problem is that you have to be lucky enough to end up in their classes (or be born in Finland). To solve the challenge of successful learning at an international level, we would need all the various education systems to be adapted according to the main discoveries in neuroscience.

Should you no longer be of school age, you may find these observations tedious. We recommend you think differently. Learning is the most crucial function of the human brain because, even if it is culturally linked to youth, it potentially never stops.

Can one learn to play a musical instrument at the age of 60? And start to speak a new language at 70? The answer is always yes—although much depends on what has happened in the previous 60 or 70 years. The more a person has increased synapses and added myelin, even past their school years, the easier learning will be for them. Somebody who has practised sport all their lives can make a golf debut when they retire, but it will be more difficult for those who've never done any sport. Similarly, those who are accustomed to reading a lot will find it easier to learn statistics or Portuguese at 60 and over. But nothing is precluded.

Words in the text: 832   *Time in seconds:* _____

ASSESSMENT

Now answer the questions below, in order, to check your comprehension and your efficiency.

1. The crazy night we spend studying before an exam:
   a) Works both in the short term and long term
   b) Works only in the short term
   c) Works especially in the long term

2. It is recommended to use the first years of our life:
   a) Going to school only, since it is already a big effort for our young brain
   b) Attending school, doing other activities and learning as much else as you can
   c) Being home-schooled, as to allow the child's brain to develop more

3. The education system that has been ranked first in the world belongs to:
   a) Canada
   b) Austria
   c) Finland

4. Your standard strict teacher and rigid exam deadlines trigger the production of:
   a) Dopamine
   b) Cortisol
   c) Serotonin

5. The critical period appropriate for experiencing a little stress is the age of:
   a) Sixteen
   b) Fifteen
   c) Eighteen

6. The only way that teachers have to trigger the circulation of dopamine, which favours and strengthens synaptic connections, is:
   a) To make their lessons fun
   b) To keep contact with the students
   c) To rearrange the classroom

7. The acetylcholine is considered to be the:
   a) Stress neuromodulator
   b) Attention neuromodulator
   c) Happiness neuromodulator

8. What is the hormone that encourages attention, and also—in the long run—attachment to studying?
   a) Noradrenaline
   b) Dopamine
   c) Oxytocin

9. Learning will be easier for a person who:
   a) Has increased synapses and added noradrenaline
   b) Has increased synapses and added dopamine
   c) Has increased synapses and added myelin

10. Teachers should not:
    a) Make their classes boring
    b) Raise their voices
    c) Threaten consequences

At this point, it is time to calculate three important factors that will give you a global understanding of your initial skills as a reader.

Words per minute (WPM): This is a measure of how quickly you have read the text. The formula to calculate it is: words in the text x 60 / time (expressed in seconds)

Write your WPM here or in your Genius Journal: 832 × 60 / _____ = _____

Immediate Recall (IR): This is a measure of how much you recall of the text you have just read, and is calculated as the percentage of how many questions you have answered correctly. Immediate Recall includes both concept- and detail-oriented questions, to test both your global understanding of the text and your ability to pick up on some details. You can find the correct answers at the end of this section.

ASSESSMENT

Write your IR here or in your Genius Journal: _____%

Efficiency: This is a value that uses your WPM and IR, as those two values taken individually will not give you an accurate picture of your reading skills. It is calculated by multiplying your WPM and your IR: so if your IR was 100% you will multiply your WPM by 1; if it was 90%, you will multiply your WPM by 0.9, and so on.

Write your Efficiency here or in your Genius Journal: _____

When looking at your numbers you may feel very happy or a bit frustrated. This is just a reminiscence of your past association with numbers. These are just numbers, and they are extremely important for your improvement—as you cannot improve what you do not measure. They are a starting point and, whether you like them or not, you will leave them in the past very quickly if you apply what you are about to read.

To improve your reading skills, there is a level you can reach without any practice (No Effort layer), by simply applying the tweaks that I will suggest. For some people this is more than enough. But if you feel you would like to take it even further, practising will be necessary (Road to Mastery layer).

Remember the concept of high-stakes and low-stakes practice? I have devised an easy way for you to be able to do both while reading this book: after all, given you are *already* reading something this book is the perfect practice for you.

At the end of each section of this book, you will find the number of words for that text. From now on, any time in which you have a chance, have a timer at hand when you read this book, applying the techniques you are about to learn and checking how fast you are going. You will notice that your speed will change according to many factors: the topic you are reading; how tired you are; whether you are using all the techniques you will read about in these chapters, or only some. But if you apply what you are about to learn, you will witness a positive trend in how fast you will be able to read the same kinds of text.

When showing you how to improve your reading speed, I am going to suggest some exercises to apply in low-stakes practice, in order to speed up faster. (You can apply these to the parts of the book that you have already read.) I will also show you some high-stakes practice, in order to use any moment in which you read as an opportunity to improve without losing your understanding. (You can apply these to the parts of the book that you have not yet read).

Answers: 1.b; 2.b; 3.c; 4.b; 5.a; 6.a; 7.b; 8.a; 9.c; 10.a

What is ahead of you
{No effort layer}

Focus

It can be easy to become distracted while reading. And it is even more frustrating when that material is important, such as revising for a test or trying to read up on a new project for work. Although you have already seen some focus techniques (Chapter Five—Create Your Momentum), you will find out about one important element that affects your concentration while reading: an apparently simple adjustment that will make a huge difference.

Speed

You are going to see some techniques that will help you increase your reading speed, allowing you to become several times faster than before. By applying this technique properly, most people read twice as fast after a few minutes; and, by doing the exercises I will suggest, they will improve further day by day.

Strategy

Not every book was created the same, so it is of utmost importance to adjust your strategy to the kind of text you have in front of you. Is it on paper or on screen? Is it a scientific article, an email, a piece of news, a novel? You will learn how to adjust your strategy according to what you have in front of you.

Retention

Putting in place all the reading techniques, not only will your Immediate Recall improve, but so will your longer-term retention (even before you apply any memory techniques!). So, fasten your seat belt: because your reading is about to be boosted!

Words: 238   *Time (in seconds):* _____

CHAPTER SEVEN

Strategy before Speed— the Five Boosters

[Bed is fine]

The first and foremost mistake that slows people down while reading is that they are too eager to go through the text. You may be wondering 'How can eagerness slow you down instead of speeding you up?', and during this chapter this is exactly what you will learn. At times in life, you need—in order to go faster—to invest some time into preparation. Reading is no exception. When you skip the steps that I am going to show you here, you may initially feel like you are saving time. However, you will later realise you will not be able to read as fast as when you do include these steps in your reading session. It is like wanting to get somewhere very fast and therefore jumping in the car and driving off, without having first checked the quickest route, and without having a satnav at your disposal. Not a smart choice.

There are five Boosters that will accelerate your reading before you even start reading the text.

The reason for this is that, regardless of what you are reading, your goal is not just to move your eyes on the page, but to understand (and at times even remember) what you are reading. The five Boosters enhance this process—so that your mind does not need to slow down as much as usual to understand what you are reading, and your tendency to distraction is tamed.

STRATEGY BEFORE SPEED—THE FIVE BOOSTERS

I will give you the full technique so that you have all the tools at hand, and can adapt them according to what you are reading (Chapter Ten—Remarks and Practice).

Words: 269   Time (in seconds): _____

Booster One: Cover
{Easy Peasy layer}

The cover of the book is the place that has the biggest impact in driving people to buy the book, yet is that which gets to be the most neglected as soon as you leave the shop.

The truth is that, once the book is in your hands, there are two kinds of feelings you may have. Either you cannot wait to dive into the first chapter (and at times you may even skip the foreword and preface to get straight to the *real* content), or—if you are reluctant to read the book because you are being made to do so—you want to get it over with as soon as you can (which, again, can lead to your ignoring the cover and skipping the pages that are numbered with Roman numerals instead of *normal* ones).

However, having a look at the cover is your first Booster, as it contains some precious pearls that will prove very helpful throughout the reading process. On the cover, you will find two fundamental pieces of information, if not more. For each piece of information, you can ask yourself different questions. At times you will know the answer; at times you will need to guess it or look it up. It does not matter if you are unsure about some of the answers, but activating your focus will work miracles for your understanding and speed (see Chapter Seven—passage on Questions).

The first piece of information will be the name of the author. This is relevant as it creates the setting for the book. Ask yourself some questions about the author:

Who are they?
What have they written before?

What background do they come from?
What is their writing style?

Then, the title. Selecting a title means squeezing the juice of the content into a few words, and to do this the author has had to choose and prioritise from the many messages that the book may contain. What is the angle the author has chosen for the book?

Why did the author select exactly those words out of the thousands that make up the text?

At times, you may find even more information on the cover. Take everything you can.

If there is an image on the cover, why that choice of image?
If there are glowing reviews, who gave them? What words did they choose?
When was the book published? Is it still current?
Is the publisher a specialised publisher?
Is the book part of a book series?

The introduction and final remarks will also be a way to enter into the author's mind; to understand the journey that led them to research and write about the specific topic, and to pinpoint their perspective and the argument they are trying to make.

A part of 'Do not judge a book by its cover' remains true, though. If it is right that the cover, introduction and final remarks will be of help to you, it is also true that they will speak for the author's mind, not yours. Once you understand where the author comes from and their point of view, then it is fundamental to read the book actively, creating your own opinion about the topic, mixing the words with your background knowledge, and asking questions with intellectual curiosity—to make sure that, by the end of the book, you are a new person.

Words: 563   *Time (in seconds):* _____

Booster Two: Preview
{Easy Peasy layer}

When you read, your mind will want to retain some of the information you encounter. But if you do not know where the text is heading, it will be very hard for you to encode and store your information so that you can recall it later (see Chapter Fourteen - Characteristics of Your Memory, to deepen the topic). Imagine that instead of living in a flat or house you live in a big room with no furniture. Imagine your memory as a huge storage room. If the storage is not organised in areas, with furniture and cabinets, you do not know where to put the information you learn: you will place it randomly in the room, but it will be extremely hard (if not impossible) for you to find the information you need at the right moment. (This is especially true if you have some specific Learning Styles).

In order to start organising your storage, I have some news that will come as a relief: you do not need to do much active work, because your mind will do it for you. Powerful thing, the brain.

The preview is divided into two phases: Overall Preview and Focused Preview.

The first one will occur at the beginning of your book; it will only be done once; and it will form the overall preview of the whole book, hence the name.

Once you open the book, your first glance should be directed at the table of contents, which will allow you to understand what the structure is (the areas and cabinets of your storage), and where to find the topics you are most interested in. The table of contents will also help you understand which chapters you can go through faster and which ones will require more attention. All you need to do is to read the contents: your mind will do the rest.

When a book is particularly thick, analysing the table of contents in the Overall Preview will be enough, else you will run the risk of overloading your mind.

The Focused Preview, instead, will be carried out at the beginning of each reading session and will only include what you will cover during that session. For example, you could do it at the beginning of each chapter.

To execute your Focused Preview properly, all you need to do is to leaf (or scroll) through the text to read all the titles, subtitles, bold characters, italics and bullet points—everything the author has decided to give more weight to. This will be very quick, but will enhance the structure your mind is creating to help you store the information.

When your author has not been so kind as to provide you with subtitles and/or bold words, you can substitute your Focused Preview with the technique we will discuss in Chapter Nine (do not worry, I'll remind you when we get there).

Disclaimer: do not apply any Preview when you are reading a novel, unless you want to spoil it.

Words: 499   *Time (in seconds):* _____

Booster Three: Goal

{Easy Peasy layer}

Imagine you are in Paris. Paris is a marvellous city, with tons of spots to visit. You are walking around and you notice a nice corner, so you stop and take a picture. Then you hear someone playing music, so you detour and stop to listen to the impromptu concert. After a few steps you notice a panoramic viewpoint, so you stop once more to take a selfie.

All of a sudden, you realise that it is the end of the day and, although your day has been amazing, you have not been to the Eiffel Tower yet! You have spent so much time chasing nice views that you got distracted. But you cannot miss the Eiffel Tower.

So, you put your blinkers on, activate your tunnel vision, speed up your walk and point at the Eiffel Tower. All the distractions that were there before suddenly seem less tempting, and you only have eyes for your goal.

It would be so great if you could have your Eiffel Tower also when reading.

Wait, you can!

All you need to do is to set a goal for the reading session. What is your intention for your session? Every text is different and for every text you will have a different goal in terms of how deep you want your retention to be. During the session, how much would you like to read and with what level of understanding?

Words: 237   Time (in seconds): _____

Booster Four: Questions

{Easy Peasy layer}

This Booster is one of my favourites, as it helps with distraction, fun, retention, understanding and speed. The truth is that when you do are not getting distracted, you are probably activating this Booster unconsciously.

Think about a novel that you have loved and that has kept you extremely engaged: one of those page-turners wherein, even if you try, you cannot seem to stop reading. Why does that happen? And how can you recreate the same level of engagement regardless of the topic you are reading?

As with everything that works, what you need to do is to analyse and discover how to replicate the same result (or similar) across other fields. Why are novels (usually) more engaging than other books? The first impulsive response you give may be related to the plot being more interesting or the style more compelling. However, this kind of answer will not help you to improve your performance, as it relates to things that you cannot change (the plot or the style of something that has already been written).

At times, in order to find a different answer, you need to ask a different question. Let's assume that the level of your engagement did not only depend on the content, but mostly on the questions you asked yourself before and while reading. I have a question for you:

what difference would you notice in the questions you ask yourself when reading something engaging and something boring?

Usually, when reading a novel, you are really immersed in the story while simultaneously your mind is often trying to guess what will happen next. Your curiosity leads you to ask unconscious questions such as 'What will happen with this character?', 'How will that character react?', 'What if he has bad intentions?', and so on.

When reading anything where this process does not happen automatically, you need to recreate the same curiosity that keeps your eyes attached to the page, looking for answers—and questions represent the perfect solution to this.

There are two kinds of questions that will increase your level of curiosity. They have different purposes, but they will both end up bringing your focus to the stars.

What do I know?—Activating your foreknowledge

With most topics, you already know much more about them than you think. You may have read about them; you may have studied them in the past or overheard someone talking about them next to you. This gives you a huge advantage, as it allows your mind to speed up and read through the bits that you already know much faster than you would otherwise. It also prevents you from wasting time re-memorising every detail you already know. There is only one problem: very often, these wonderful advantages are never activated. The reason is that if you do not activate your foreknowledge then your mind will find it impossible to capitalise on it. It is like having a promo code and not using it.

Activating your foreknowledge is as simple as this: look at the title and subtitles and ask yourself what you already know about the topic. If there is a lot that you already know, you can quickly mind map your foreknowledge (for mind maps, see Chapter Thirteen). If, instead, you do not know much, or you are reading for pleasure and not for studying, you will not need to note it down.

What do I want to know?—Be like Sherlock

The second kind of question is directed not to your foreknowledge but to your future knowledge. I have always been fascinated by anything Sherlock Holmes-related, and this is one of those instances in which I get to feel like Holmes for a moment. What you need to ask yourself is 'What do I want to know about this topic?' Using the Wh- questions of journalism, you can ask yourself what you want to investigate, and—very importantly—make an accurate guess about the answers, even when you have no clue what they could be.

This has a double advantage. On one level there is a part of your brain that is called the RAS (Reticular Activating System), which has the role of filtering the inputs you receive from the exterior so that your brain will not be overloaded. By asking these questions, you will ensure your RAS is ready to filter the knowledge you are seeking rather than overlooking it.

The second advantage is that everyone—yourself included—wants to be right. So after guessing your answer one of these two things will happen while you are reading: either you will be proven correct in your guess (and so you will remember the answer because you are happy you were right), or you will be proven incorrect in your guess (and so you will remember the answer because it is different from what you had thought it would be). This process will keep you much more engaged and will increase your retention immediately.

There are several ways to ask yourself what you want to know, and some texts will help you more than others. If you have an abstract at the beginning of the chapter, subheadings throughout, or questions at the end of the chapter, all these things will be a great prompt. When you are left with less cues as to what is relevant in the chapter, what you can do is to utilise what you have at your disposal. After your Focused Preview, you will have some questions to start with, whether it is on a title or from the alternative preview that I will explain in Chapter Nine. For example, if your title is 'The process of putting first things first', what you will try to guess may be: 'What can you consider as "first things"?'; 'How can you put them first?'; 'What do you do with what you do not put first?'; 'If it is a process, are there different steps?'; and so on. Asking questions (and making accurate guesses) is an art that will increase your curiosity, attention and retention immensely, and it can be a lot of fun to practise!

Words: 1,022   Time (in seconds): _____

Booster Five: Flow
{No effort layer}

The fifth Booster to improve your reading speed and retention lies in improving your focus. If you have already read Part I, about Preparation (especially Chapter Five—Momentum), you are already familiar with some techniques that will help you enter into a flow state. This makes a difference between reading a text once and retaining most of what you are reading and needing to re-read it several times because your mind was somewhere else.

So as a Booster, just remember to put your posture in place, enter a flow state and enjoy.

Words: 93   Time (in seconds): _____

CHAPTER EIGHT

When Your Goal Is to Understand

[Desk is better]

Now that you have used your Boosters, it is time to read.

Subvocalisation and Regressions
{No effort layer}

One of the most common questions I hear about reading is: How can I remove subvocalisation? If you are not familiar with the term, subvocalisation represents saying the words that you are reading, either out loud or in your mind; and, in most texts about speed-reading, it is described as *the* obstacle you need to overcome to be able to read faster. It is true that the spoken language is far slower than your mind's ability to process what you are reading—and so focusing on the voice that is reading the words inside your head will definitely slow you down.

However, I have some good and bad news for you. The bad news is that for most people it will prove impossible to silence the voice completely. The good news is that you do not need to silence it in order to read fast—instead simply lower its volume and go so fast that it cannot keep up with your speed. Focusing on what you are reading rather than what you are hearing will be easier than you think, and will allow you to flow through the page at a speed that your voice would not be able to keep up with! There will be some exercises that I will suggest for your skimming abilities, and as a by-product they too will help you to ignore the voice (see Chapter Nine—passage on Skimming).

The other hotly debated aspect of speed-reading concerns regressions. Regressions are those movements that you make by going back to re-read words that you have already read. It has been proven that, on most of the occasions in which you go back to re-read a concept, you are not actually understanding more than the first time you read it, yet you keep doing so because it makes you feel safer.

I have read articles and books insisting that you should get rid of regressions, and others that state that if we tend to regress it is because we need it. As usual, I believe that balance and flexibility are the key, and during this chapter you will see where balance can be found.

Words: 381 *Time (in seconds): _____*

Critical Reading
{Easy Peasy layer}

Meet your Ally

In this part I am going to introduce the best ally that you will have any time you need to read. It is going to help you to reduce subvocalisation and regressions; to read much faster without yet practising any techniques; to keep your focus higher; and to keep your process of improvement active over time. That is why it is unmissable.

Its name is the Pointer (aka Tracker, aka Pacer).

The Pointer was born out of a simple concept: when you learn how to read, your first instinct is to point at the words with your finger; and, as you grow, you will still find yourself pointing at words when scrolling through a list or searching for a word in a dictionary. The reason is that guiding your sight with an external support (a finger) helps direct your focus to what you really want. When you use a Pointer in the right way, you will see your speed increasing instantaneously.

The technique is simple. Take a pen (with its cap on) or a chopstick (chopsticks are my favourites) and underline each word on the line as you read. You can imagine that the words are birds, you are a birdwatcher and the Pointer is your binoculars. Your goal is to follow the birds as they are flying, with a smooth movement. There is one rule: the Pointer never goes back.

Do not go from the first word of the line to the last, as that will waste some time for you. Your eyes see more than just one word at every fixation, so starting from the first word would mean wasting part of your field of perception on the empty margins. Initially you can point from the second word until the second to last. As you do the exercise that I will suggest later in this chapter, you will be able to begin from word three, four or five. You will notice that it will also depend on the size of the book, the font that is used, how far the book is from your eyes, and so on—so *flexibility* is necessary.

Highest Speed vs Perfect+1 Speed

There are two kinds of speed you can keep when using your Pointer. The first speed is the Highest speed practice, and you will use it as an exercise to enhance your improvement. As the name suggests, it needs to be applied to Low-Stakes Practice material, for example all the pages of this book that you have already read. Given that you have already understood the concepts in them, it will not be a problem when initially you will not understand the meaning of what you are reading.

For this kind of practice, you will be reading extremely fast (at least one line per second), and you will proceed along the page. Your goal will not be to understand what you are reading (and do not expect to be understanding anything the first times), but by keeping your speed high your mind will start perceiving more and more words and blocks of words, until your comprehension starts to improve.

After working with the Highest speed practice, you will notice that, even when slowing down to reach your Perfect+1 speed, you will be much faster than before.

The second speed is the Perfect+1 speed. This will be your default reading speed any time you are reading something you need to understand (High Stakes Practice material). By applying the Pointer (and all the Boosters) you will notice you will go much faster than before. Not only is this speed sustainable and zero-risk, but it will also allow you to keep improving your speed *every time* you are reading anything.

To reach your Perfect+1 speed, what you need to do is to read the text with your Pointer at a comfortable speed that allows you to easily understand what you are reading. At that point, do +1 (as shown in Chapter Three). Ask yourself to read one more word than is comfortable. It needs to feel 'just too uncomfortable'—this alertness will help you keep your attention high. If you were in a situation in which you needed to drive home at night and you were pretty tired, what would be safer: going very slowly or a bit faster than usual? The latter: because this would keep your senses active. In a similar way, your Perfect+1 speed will help you keep alert and understand even more than if you were going very slowly.

How to improve immediately

From now on, every time you read, make sure you use your Pointer. You will see that the more you use it, the less you will want to be without it. Whenever you can (I do not expect you to do it all the time, but even once in a while would already be great), use a stopwatch to monitor how long it takes you to read a paragraph. At the end of each paragraph you will find how many words it includes, and by applying the formula you learned in Chapter Seven, WPM = Words x 60 / Time, you will be able to calculate how many words per minute you have read. As a scientist, note down anything you may find relevant. Were you tired or rested? Were you focused or distracted? Did you apply all the Boosters or just some? What time of day is it?

All this information will turn out to be extremely helpful in getting to know yourself better and tweaking what needs to be tweaked.

Is slow better?

At times people have the misconception that if they go slow they will understand more. It is an understandable belief, but think about this.
If I write like this is itea si er or
harder to understand what I am writing? If your mind needs to wait a while before putting all the pieces together, your processing will be harder. So, if it is true that you need to find a balance between speed and understanding, very often this balance will not be found by going slowly.

After you have practised a bit...

Remember when I said you should never go back with the Pointer? Well, this is only partly true. Initially you need to force your mind and eyes into the habit of moving forward so that you can counterbalance the habit of regressions. Your mind should know that you are not going back unless it is strictly necessary, so that your level of attention will be increased.

However, I am of the opinion that this should be taken to the extreme. I have witnessed people who would not let themselves regress even if not understanding that paragraph meant they would not then understand the following two chapters. This is not necessary (and not that useful for the purpose you have while reading).

While going back is a waste of time when it is recurring too frequently and is due to a lack of focus, it is perfectly fine when at the end of a paragraph you realise that you have not understood something.

Once you have practised a bit with the Smooth Pointer technique, you can try out the Jumping Pointer technique. This is a technique in which instead of underlining words with your Pointer, you use it to point at two or three spots on each line: as if you were jumping from one block of words to another. For certain kinds of texts, I find the Jumping Pointer to be my favourite technique, as it helps me to keep a rhythm that I would not otherwise have.

How to improve with the Jumping Pointer
{Road to Mastery layer}

There are a lot of exercises you can do to improve your eye movements. One that will help you both with your speed and with the technique of the Jumping Pointer consists of practising with a metronome. Metronomes are used mostly by musicians and logopedists as they produce beats at the interval of your choosing, but they also turn out to be very helpful for reading improvement. Set the bpm (beats per minute) to one hundred and ninety. You will hear very quick beats. You need to imagine that on each line there are three dots: one a couple of words from the beginning, one in the middle and one a couple of words from the end of the line. Your goal will be to move your eyes from one imaginary dot to the next at each beat of the metronome.

Initially this may be extremely difficult, and you may not understand much. So when you do it as an exercise, do it with Low-Stakes practice so that you do not need to bother about understanding.

As you do it a few times, you will notice how you will start picking up more and more words, until you soon realise that you are understanding most of the text. At that point, raise the bpm. This exercise will help you go so much faster without even realising, and, as a by-product, it will also help reduce your subvocalisation immensely.

Words: 1,545   *Time (in seconds):* _____

CHAPTER NINE

When Your Goal Is not to Understand

[Bed is fine]

Reading this chapter heading you may think 'Well, when I read I always want to understand, didn't you say that understanding is fundamental?'

It is. However, there may be times in which your purpose when reading is not to understand everything. Instead, it may be to find a piece of information hidden in the ocean of words; to re-read something that you have already read; or to find a way to do your Focused Preview (Chapter Seven) when there are no subheadings to help you.

For these purposes, you will use two different kinds of reading: skimming and scanning.

Words: 100   Time (in seconds): _____

Skimming
{Easy Peasy layer}

Skimming consists of reading through the text very quickly in order to get the overall idea. Your focus while skimming is not to comprehend, but to activate the side of your brain that is able to take pictures of what you are reading so it can then put them together. Think about it as creating a trailer of what is in the text.

Your first instinct when skimming will be to *read* word by word, but you need to imagine your eyes are a camera taking a lot of shots of every point you lay them on, rather than stopping to integrate each word inside your brain.

The speed should be very fast (1,000 WPM and upwards), and the movement of your eyes can be either of the three below. (I would suggest that you do not use a Pointer for this kind of reading, but that you let your eyes free to wander on the page.)

On some texts, reading the first and last sentence of each paragraph will allow you to absorb all you need for your skimming, maybe even more.

On some other texts you may want to follow a precise pattern, to give yourself a repetitive rhythm that will allow you not to think about where to go next. For example, you could move along a diagonal pattern from left to right (or vice versa) along the page, or an S pattern, or a spiral pattern.

On other texts you will prefer to move your eyes randomly, wherever you feel they should go.

Regardless of what pattern you follow, remember that your purpose is to acquire a general idea of the topic rather than understand everything. When you apply skimming in conjunction with the Boosters (Chapter Seven), you will be able to create an idea of up to thirty per cent of the text. If you understand more, go faster!

This will be especially helpful when it is not possible to apply a Focused Preview. This could happen in texts with no subheadings, where you want to create that initial structure we spoke about; but also in emails or articles that you want to skim before deciding whether to invest more time to actually read them.

How to improve your skimming ability
{Road to Mastery layer}

There are several ways to improve your ability to photograph words and retain them. One simple strategy is to use apps like Spreeder, where you can select how many words you want to be shown at once. They will be shown at the appropriate speed for you to go beyond subvocalisation and still understand the text.

Words: 436   *Time (in seconds):* _____

Scanning
{Easy Peasy layer}

Another kind of reading that you may need to do more often than you think is called scanning. This allows you to quickly run your eyes over the page to find some specific information.

You may need to scan when you have some specific questions you are required to answer, or when you have applied Booster Four (Questions) very well; you may be reading an email looking for that one piece of information that you need, or you may be looking for where in the text a certain topic will be covered.

Regardless of the reason for your scanning, all you need to do is to make sure you have a clear idea of what you are looking for, and then run your eyes over the page, ignoring everything that is not the word you need. Your eyes have a special ability to find what they are looking for, and that is why Booster Four is so effective. After you find what you are looking for, always read what is around the word or block of words you identified, to ensure you actually found the right answer.

How to improve your scanning skills
{Road to Mastery layer}

An exercise you can do in order to improve your scanning skills is to have a page in front of you and then ask someone to tell you a group of three words you need to find on the page. Do your best to find them as quickly as possible, and then repeat this exercise using other sets of words.

Initially you can practise with things that are easier to find, such as numbers, capitalised words, weird names and similar. As you become better and better, you can practise on plainer information and smaller fonts, which will be harder to spot.

If you do not have anyone to help you, you can copy a page and cut it into pieces showing two-to-three words each, which you can then shuffle and pick out. Although this will require more time to prepare, it will allow you more autonomy to practise.

Words: 347 *Time (in seconds):* _____

CHAPTER TEN

Remarks and Practice

[Desk is better]

There is a word that I have already mentioned a few times and that you will encounter many more times in the book: flexibility.

All of us are wired extremely differently, and it would be crazy to believe that the exact same strategy that works for you will work for your friend or partner. It is paramount that you experiment. (And if you are interested in developing your learning method further, I would suggest you take me up on my earlier offer of a surprise gift that you can find at geniusbychoice.co.uk/gift.)

Even if you decided not to use your access to the gift, please remember to experiment and try everything on yourself before setting anything in stone. When reading, there are two variables you need to keep in mind. These are that the texts themselves will vary, and the devices you read them on will change.

For how to approach the different types of text I will spend few words: as you can find all the information you need in the previous chapters. However, I really want to emphasise how the Boosters will help you clarify the purpose of your reading, and therefore adjust the strategy you adopt. When reading an email, an online post, a scientific article, a novel, a personal development book, a text you are studying, a script you need to memorise, or any other text, your strategy will need to be slightly (or very) different.

Words: 268   Time (in seconds): _____

Reading fast in a technological world
{No Effort layer}

Reading on paper and reading on screen may share some common elements, but they also have some differences you will want to keep in mind, especially when it comes to the eye fatigue you may experience.

The first thing you will want to adjust when reading on screen is to increase the frequency of your breaks. Your eye strain will be higher than when reading on paper, so you will undertake your assessment every fifteen minutes instead of every twenty-five (see Chapter Five—passage on Study Cycles).

As far as the Pointer goes, while it is possible to use your cursor or a pen when reading on a monitor, it will be harder and at times impossible to do so when reading on your phone. Do not despair: there are other ways to make you fast. A phone screen has less width than a book page or a monitor, so your eyes will have much less further to travel across the screen. What I love to do is to keep my thumbs on both sides of the screen in order to mark where I am, as it helps me guide my reading, and ensures I keep track and go fast.

Words: 208　　　　　　　　　　Time (in seconds): _____

Practice

{Easy Peasy layer}

Here you will find another test you can take. Apply everything we have discussed and you will see how, even if you have not practised much yet, your results will already be different!

Imagination—Extract from *The Brain: A User's Manual* by Marco Magrini

Wherever you may be at this moment, you have a clear perception of your environment and surrounding events. Let's do an experiment. Imagine that three Wild West cowboys suddenly appear in front of you, or three film celebrities and try to imagine what will happen in the next 30 seconds.

Did the cowboys start shooting? Did Julia Roberts come down and sit next to you? Whatever happened, your brain has drawn a parallel reality, generated by divergent thinking, or the choice from many possible alternatives. The perfect example of this process is that demonstrated by Albert Einstein, who, drawing on his breadth of knowledge, his deep curiosity about the unknown, and well-focused attention on the problems of the universe, discovered that time and space are different dimensions of the same spatiotemporal continuum.

But this is an inappropriate example, because it gives the sense that imagination is the exclusive preserve of Nobel Prize winners, when it is actually available to the entire human race. It's about drawing in your mind an alternative road to escape the traffic. It's writing poems to flirt with someone. It's inventing a new fusion recipe. But it's also the door to creativity, usually defined as the production of original ideas that have an intrinsic value. Just like the arrow, the anchor and the anvil.

In post-industrial society, creativity has become classified as an essential economic resource. In 2011, the total sum of publishing, arts, design, fashion, film, music, TV shows and software represented roughly 3% of European GDP, 500 billion euros, and six million jobs. It has grown substantially since then, According to economists, creativity is destined to have an increasingly key role in global economic competition, because responses to modern challenges are shaped, at times even more than by the price, by the strength and novelty of ideas.

The so-called 'knowledge economy' is a new industry that isn't—like so many industries before it—based on the strength of muscles or machine, but on that of divergent thinking. It's called 'knowledge' because it includes patents, trade secrets and various types of expertise, but we could also call it creativity economics because the starting and end point are valuable creations. It's hard to say when it began (long before the invention of the printing press?), but it has, for sure, a great deal of time before it expands, changes and increases its hold over the world now that digital communication has allowed us to cross geographical and temporal barriers. Just to be clear, the knowledge economy is the reason that, on Wall Street in September 2018, Alphabet Inc. (Google) was worth more than seven Fords, General Motors and Chryslers put together. From this early glimpse of the 21st century, it is clear that creativity is the most strategic economic resource there is. Which is why it is perfectly sensible to learn to cultivate it. Every brain is equipped with an integrated system, made up of many different areas that become active whenever the user shifts his or her attention from the outside to the inside world. Discovered in 2001, the default mode network—the 'start-up' mode of brain mechanism—is at the neural root of reflective thinking, be it in relation to oneself or to others, the memory of the past or the forecast of the future. To be precise, it is active when your mind drifts, when you daydream. And, consequently, also when you use your imagination to climb the high peaks of creativity.

The default mode network includes numerous and assorted areas of the brain, which have close axonic contact between them. As always happens in the most complex executive functions, the prefrontal cortex is significantly involved in the mechanism. However, parts of the cingulate cortex, which is collocated between the corpus callosum of the temporal and parietal lobes, are also involved, as in the hippocampus. It must be mentioned that the default mode network also plays a part in self-awareness and consciousness.

As people accustomed to creating and inventing know, that particular state of mind connected to abstraction and divergent thinking is reached through a peculiar kind of concentration that opens up the prairie of imagination. It's almost like a click that switched on the brain's creative mode. In her book *A Mind for Numbers,* Barbara Oakley, Professor of Engineering at Oakland University, calls it the diffuse mode. In a nutshell, the 'diffuse mode' consists of a 'diffuse' thought, capable of observing all the aspects of a problem, and is typical associated with the default mode network, as opposed to the 'focused mode', which is the rational and analytic attention of the prefrontal cortex. No brain, not even yours, is capable of activating both systems at the same time. The methods currently adopted (including by multinational companies) for developing imagination are abundant and varied, because there isn't just one creativity model. Each of us can legitimately find our own formula, in tune with our particular passions or inclinations; all we need is to know that it can truly fuel us.

Words in the text: 837 *Time in seconds:* _____

1. Albert Einstein discovered that:
    a) Time and space are different dimensions of the same spatiotemporal continuum
    b) Time and space are the same dimension of a different spatiotemporal continuum
    c) Time and space are the same dimension of the same spatiotemporal continuum

2. Imagination is:
    a) Exclusive to geniuses and Nobel Prize winners
    b) Available to all humans
    c) Available to those humans who learn from geniuses and Nobel Prize winners

3. In post-industrial society, creativity has become classified as:
    a) An essential economic resource
    b) A non-essential economic resource
    c) An essential social resource

4. In _____ the total sum of publishing, arts, design, fashion, film, music, TV shows and software represented roughly 3% of European GDP, 500 billion euros, and six million jobs:
   a) 2001
   b) 2011
   c) 2017

5. According to economists, creativity is destined to have an increasingly key role in global economic competition, because responses to modern challenges are shaped, at times even more than by the price, by:
   a) The strength and novelty of ideas
   b) The speed in coming up with ideas
   c) The variety of ideas

6. The so-called 'knowledge economy' is based on:
   a) Divergent thinking
   b) The strength of muscles or machine
   c) The collection of all the knowledge available to mankind

7. The default mode network is active when:
   a) You are totally focused
   b) You are asleep
   c) Your mind drifts

8. Which part of the brain is not mentioned to have a significant role in the default mode network?
   a) The prefrontal cortex
   b) The cingulate cortex
   c) The amygdala

9. Divergent thinking happens at the moment in which we have:
   a) A 'diffuse' thought, capable of observing all the aspects of a problem
   b) A 'focused' thought, which is the rational and analytic attention of the prefrontal cortex
   c) A thought that is partly 'diffuse' and partly 'focused'

10. Talking about the methods currently adopted for developing imagination, we can say that:
    a) Each of us can legitimately find our own formula, in tune with our particular passions or inclinations
    b) They all converge into one unique formula, which puts together the best strategies to develop imagination
    c) They are still being developed as nothing seems to be working to create an effective formula

Write your WPM here or in your Genius Journal: 837 x 60 / _____ = _____

Write your IR here or in your Genius Journal: _____%
(You can find the correct answers at the end of this section)

Write your Efficiency here or in your Genius Journal: _____

You may have improved your Words per minute, your Immediate recall, both, or none. It does not matter. If you are happy with your result, give yourself a moment to acknowledge your improvement. But do not rest on your laurels—there is so much you can still improve.

If you are a bit disappointed with your score, ask yourself to use your scientific mind to understand what you can do better. Maybe you tried to go too fast for your understanding? Or too slow? Maybe you did not use the Pointer, or maybe you were too focused on doing well rather than on the text itself?

Analyse it with a critical eye that will help you to adjust and improve. And remember: every paragraph will have the number of words noted down at the end, so you can keep practising and improving while reading this book!

Answers: 1.a; 2.b; 3.a; 4.b; 5.a; 6.a; 7.c; 8.a; 9.a; 10.a

Inspiration Time from Our Genius Alumni

I am a student at Tulane University in New Orleans, Louisiana USA, and I am studying abroad at the London School of Economics for this academic year. I found Genius in 21 Days through the LSE societies fair; their banner about improving your reading speed and learning foreign languages faster intrigued me.

After attending a free taster session, I decided that it was imperative that I take the course for myself. The days following the course, I immediately started implementing what I had learned: I changed the way I take notes in class, I started learning 30 Spanish words a day, and I started applying speed reading techniques.

My new note-taking method allowed me to understand "one of the toughest economic models we have done so far" (according to my lecturer) and see how certain factors affected other factors in this model with ease while my classmates were not able grasp a generic example of what we had just learned during that class.

I took a trip to Barcelona 2 weekends after I took this course. As a result of learning, and memorizing, 30 Spanish words per day, I was able to talk around 40-50% Spanish with friends that I made there on my previous trip - granted it was broken Spanish because I have not started learning grammar yet, but it was better than anything I could have done without the techniques for learning a foreign language.

My favorite result, however, is my reading speed. I used to think I was a slow reader, and during the course my reading speed prior to learning the techniques was 172 words per minute. After learning and implementing the techniques, my fastest three recorded reading speeds have been 1040, 1100, and 1137 words per minute. I used another reading technique to read through a 235 page book in just 20 minutes!

I am absolutely amazed with the results I have achieved only one month after taking the course, and I hope the story of my growth and progress aids you in making what I believe should be an easy decision: take the Genius in 21 Days course to discover a world of growth, motivation, and learning that would be extremely difficult to find without their techniques and desire to help you.

Zachin Rao - University Student

PART III.
INTERNALISE

Internalising is the process of taking the information that is coming from the exterior (a book, a lecture, a video, a podcast…) and making it your own, integrating the new information with your previous knowledge to create something new.

One of the main problems that you need to face when you study a text is that the language used to write the text is not the same as the language your mind uses to understand and process information.

However, when you realise that the text you are studying is written in the same language you will be using when you need to express it, you may easily fall into a trap.

Text

Expression

Why do I say 'trap'? Because this similarity between text and expression creates an almost irresistible temptation for most students: to study the text in the same language they will use to express it.

This does not work! The reason is very simple. Our mind speaks a different language to that of written and spoken ones. It is like if you read a text in Finnish (without knowing the language) and you memorised it as it is written without translating it. You cannot expect to understand it and be able to reason about it if you have not translated it first. The gaps in your preparation will be huge. And if this was not enough, it will be much harder for you to memorise what you need.

Fortunately, there is a simple way to avoid all of this and ensure that your preparation is deep, accurate and even faster. Are you ready?

The image we are going to use is the hourglass.

Why an hourglass? Because the language of our mind works in a similar way. You cannot let all the sand (the information) in at once; you need to filter it. This process happens in the de-coding phase.

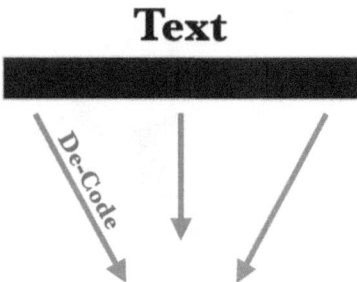

Only once you have simplified the pieces of information so that they can go through the neck of the hourglass will you possess the ability to understand and process them.

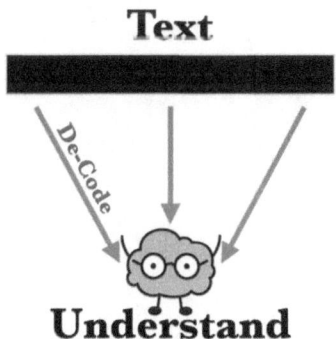

At this point, re-coding the pieces of information to be able to express them will be child's play—much simpler than memorising an entire text in a language that, in fact, does not belong to your brain.

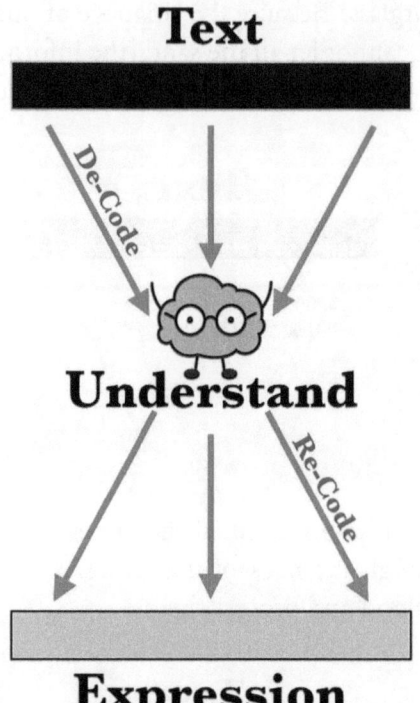

Ready to start?

Words: 382   Time (in seconds): _____

CHAPTER ELEVEN

Decoding and Understanding

[Bed is fine]

Talking about processing will necessarily lead to discussing other study phases that have an irrefutable influence on your processing ability. If some of the phases I will mention are not clear, make sure to read the chapters where we outline them in greater depth.

When you read a text, one of the main mistakes that lead to distraction (and hence a difficulty in understanding) is reading passively without interacting with the text. We have discussed this concept when talking about Strategic Reading, but it will serve as helpful here too.

The question I want to ask you is: when you have a page in front of you, how is it structured?

HEADING

<u>Subheading</u>

_____
_____
_____
_____

_ _ _ _ _ _ _ _ _ _ _
_ _ _ _ _ _ _ _ _ _ _

_____
_____
_____

_ _ _ _ _ _ _ _ _ _ _
_ _ _ _ _ _ _ _ _ _ _

Every text is divided into chapters, subchapters (at times sub-sub-chapters) and paragraphs. This subdivision is not casual, and it will turn out to be very helpful when you need to decode the text.

Every author chooses to start a new line for a new point because it represents—according to the author's personal processing—the end of one concept and the beginning of another. This gives you a huge hint: paragraphs will be the 'unit of measurement' of the text, the foundation on which you will lay your work.

Here below you will find the steps to follow for each paragraph. Remember that at the beginning of each subchapter, it will be fundamental to apply the Strategic Reading techniques described in Chapter Six.

Here are the eight steps of internalising: the ones that will lead you to the other bulb of the hourglass. The first two will allow you to understand the text; steps three to seven to process the information; and step 8 to organise it according to how your brain thinks.

Words: 287   Time (in seconds): _____

Hourglass One: Read
{Easy Peasy layer}

Critical Reading of the Paragraph.
   First of all, read the paragraph with your Pointer (see Chapter Eight).

Hourglass Two: Child
{Easy Peasy layer}

At the end of a paragraph, stop and ask yourself: 'Could I explain it to a kid?' This process leads you to simplify the concept as much as you can, so that someone who does not have your foreknowledge can also understand it. In order to explain it to a child, you need to break the concept down into simpler ones—and this is what will help the information pass through the neck of the hourglass.
   If your answer to this question is: 'Yes, I would be able to explain it clearly to a kid', move on to Hourglass Three.
   If, on the other hand, you find it hard to explain the content of the paragraph in simple terms, it means that there are some gaps in your understanding. There may be several reasons for this.
   Regardless of the reason, it is necessary for you to take measures to bridge those gaps.
   Here are three steps that you can follow in that case.

'It's not your intelligence,...

a)... it's your Lack of Focus!'

At times the answer is simpler than you expect. And on occasion the sole reason you have not understood a text is that your mind was elsewhere. So, the first step when you do not understand a paragraph is to re-read the paragraph, to make sure that your lack of understanding does not stem from a lack of concentration.

b)... it's your Lack of Vocabulary!'

When re-reading is not enough, it means that there is another factor that is preventing you from understanding. Your goal will be to find out what it is. (And you are not allowed to conclude 'I just do not understand this topic'.)

One of the main contributing factors to your lack of understanding is your lack of vocabulary.

For this reason, when re-reading is not enough, what you need to do is to search for two kinds of words in the text: words that you do not know, and words that you think you know.

The words that you do not know are very easy to find. It is those words that you stumble over, because when your mind reads them it finds no reference in your knowledge.

The words that you think you know are less easy to find, as when you look at them you may feel you know what they mean. So how can you recognise them? You can recognise them by the fact that you would not be able to define them clearly. Here is an example: the word 'inflation'. Almost everyone has an idea of what 'inflation' means, but fewer people are able to describe its implications. Therefore, when you find it in a text, you may move past it—thinking that you have understood the text—only to find yourself puzzled later, because the author, by using the word 'inflation', was implying a series of consequences that will be taken for granted in the text (but which you are not aware of) and therefore expose some gaps in your understanding.

When you find words that you do not know (from either category), it is important to search for their meaning in a dictionary, so that you can enrich your vocabulary and increase your understanding.

c)... it's your Language!'

If after looking for the words you did not know you still do not understand what the text is saying, the reason probably lies in the fact that the author's language is really tough to decode.

What can you do in this case?

Rely on technology! Nowadays, using Google, you can find almost any concept expressed in simpler terms or in a way that is more aligned with your pre-knowledge and your cognitive styles. So, this step consists of doing an online search to find an article or a video that explains the concept in simpler terms.

After this, go back to your paragraph: you will see that it will be less obscure, and probably even easy to understand!

d)...it's your Background Knowledge!

If, after simplifying the language of the paragraph, your understanding is still poor, then only one explanation remains: your background knowledge on the topic is not strong enough. For example, if I wanted to explain hard maths concepts to you, but you had not yet learnt the basic principles, then everything would look hard.

So, the last step is to grow your background knowledge. I will warn you: this is the final step because hopefully you will only need to do it rarely, as it takes longer than the other ones.

How do you build background knowledge? Identify the building blocks of the topic (having a look at vocabulary again will help), and make sure that you do not only understand what each word means, but that your background knowledge on each sub-concept is very strong. You cannot build a solid building if the foundation is not there!

And remember: 'It's not your intelligence, it's your strategy!'

Words: 828   *Time (in seconds): _____*

CHAPTER TWELVE

Processing

[Desk is better]

Hourglass Three: Do I need it?

{Easy Peasy layer}

After ensuring you have understood, ask yourself the question: 'Do I need this paragraph?'

There are times in which the paragraph is only introductory, is redundant, or is useless with regards to your goal. In such case, your job for that paragraph is done, and you can start again from step one (Critical reading) with the following paragraph.

If instead you need to remember its content in the future, go to step four.

Words: 82   *Time (in seconds):* _____

Hourglass Four: Label

{Easy Peasy layer}

Imagine you are moving house. It is an accurate analogy because processing is that phase that will allow you to 'move' the concepts from the text to your mind. When moving house you need to deal with a large number of boxes, represented here by the paragraphs. Now imagine if, while moving, you had a series of boxes without labels. It would be very hard to put them in the right place! So, what would you need to do? You would need to open each box and decide how to label it, so that when you looked at it later you would know immediately where it should go.

When reading, after understanding the concept of the paragraph, this is the first thing to do: put a label on the paragraph, to make sure you know what is inside.

What is a label?

A label is the 'title' that you choose to give to the paragraph. The rationale is the following: if the author has decided to group these sentences and then begin a new paragraph, it means that there is a common element, a category, a classification, something that distinguishes this paragraph from the previous one and from the following one. What is the common element or the category?

Write the label alongside the text to make its revision simple.

For example, in the subchapter the author could be talking about all the reasons that led to the beginning of the Second World War, while in the paragraph they could talk specifically about the political causes. Your label of the paragraph could be 'Political'. (I use the word 'could' because keywords and labels are extremely personal, and so some words I would choose could be different from yours.)

WORLD WAR II

<u>Cause</u>

POLITICAL

Words: 288   *Time (in seconds): _____*

Hourglass Five: Keywords and details
{Easy Peasy layer}

This is an optional phase, because at times the label will be enough. Other times, however, there may be more complex paragraphs where, in addition to the label, there are concepts to remember that are lower in 'hierarchy' but still important to know.

So, once you have chosen the label, identify if there are concepts that hierarchically are in a lower position inside the paragraph, and whether the paragraph contains any details you need to highlight. For the concepts: write down a keyword that triggers them, and circle it. For the details: mark those you wish to remember by underlining them.

The distinction between keywords and details, although not always strict, is fundamental to keep in mind.

A keyword represents a concept that I can express with my own words, while a detail is something I need to record as it is (facts, names, dates, figures). To create a keyword from a concept, you need to understand the concept and 'squeeze' it. To find a detail, you just need to ask yourself whether you want to retain that detail or not (at times texts are full of details that are almost useless for you, so you will not select them).

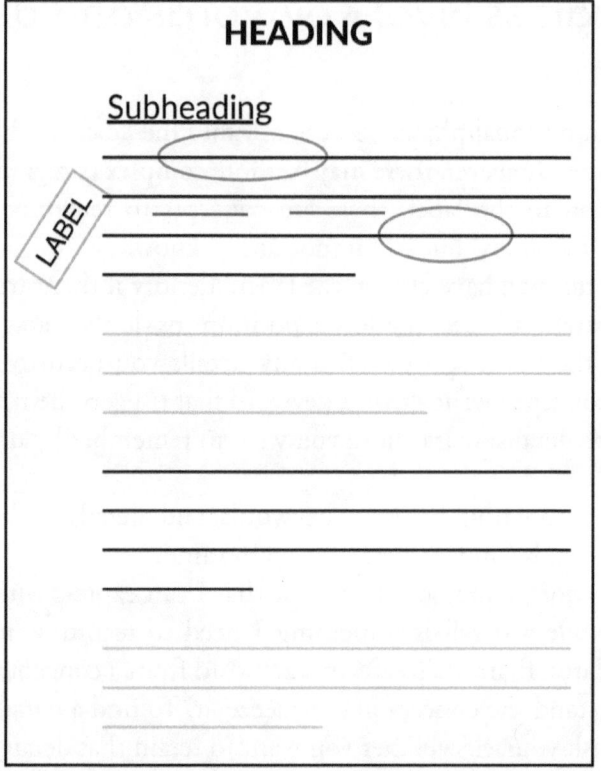

How can you find an effective label/keyword?

A label is basically a keyword (or better, a super-keyword), so I will treat labels and keywords in the same way in this section, as their characteristics are the same.

I do not know if you have ever worked with keywords, but most people who have do not have a great relationship with them.

I am no different. At least, I was not before. I remember my first real experience with keywords: I was in middle school, and my teacher had told us that to study better we should look out for the keywords that would be listed at the end of each chapter. I was a very diligent girl, and I tried my best effort to compile what I thought would be the keywords from the text. But, when I came to the small box at the end of the chapter that: 'The keywords of this chapter are...', I found that—every single time—my keywords would not match those provided by the author. How do you think my mind then reacted—'This keywords thing is not for me'. And I stopped my search for keywords, returning to my old method that, although maybe not perfect, at least worked for me.

When I took the Genius in 21 Days course at age eighteen, I finally realised that the problem was not me (which was a good boost for my confidence, especially in my ability to process the information I was reading).

The fact is that the first main characteristic of keywords is that they are subjective. I could read the same page as you and we could come up with completely different keywords. This would not make your or my keywords wrong. It would simply reflect how we process information differently; that some words are more evocative for you than for me, and vice versa.

The reason I had stopped using keywords in middle school was because I felt I was doing it wrong, and that—just by looking at the keywords that the author had selected—I was unable to come up with all the things I should remember. I did not feel safe in relying solely on keywords.

How many times have I heard people say that the only reason why they were not favouring keywords over whole sentences was because they were afraid keywords would not be enough...

To be honest, this is completely understandable. Because of the way we have been taught, we go from text to expression, trying to remember as much as possible without having processed the information. Of course, when there is no processing work taking place, the only thing you can rely on is to select as many words as you can so you will be able to repeat them and memorise them. However, trying to commit all those words to memory without having processed the information will be an exhausting job. We have all been there.

With the Hourglass Technique, I am asking you to enter an utterly different world. You will no longer be jumping from text to expression, trying to remember things by *repeating repeating repeating*, but instead you will be processing the information so that it can really go through the hourglass smoothly. Once you understand a concept and you come up with a keyword to represent it, you do not need all the other words. All you need are that one keyword and those ancillary details that you will also be selecting as you go. Your mind knows how to talk about a concept without you needing to repeat the exact same words that someone else is using in order to express it. So instead of having sentences and sentences to memorise, you will just have a few words: your mind will have absorbed the concepts behind those words already.

I also have some more good news for you! When you select your keyword, you do not have to remember the concept behind it forever. You just need to remember it for one hour. If after one hour you see that by looking at your keyword you are still able to come up with the concept, then your work is done. This is because in Chapter Nineteen we are going to see how to commit memory to the long term. For now trust me: one hour is all you need.

Now that you have seen how the keywords that are right for you will make your life easier and your learning faster, it is time to answer a very important question: how do you know if a keyword is right for you?

Keywords, not key sentences.

A keyword may involve one word, at times a couple of words, but never a sentence. Why? Because of our hourglass. If you select a whole sentence, how can it go down the neck to the other bulb? You need to break the concept down and ask yourself: 'What is THE word that will trigger the whole concept for me?'

Of course, flexibility is paramount. I have read in certain books how a keyword should never include more than one word. Well, I believe that this depends. For example, think about the word 'time'. In itself it triggers a certain concept. Think about the word 'management'. On its own it takes your mind to certain ideas. But when you put them together, you have a whole new concept: 'time management'. In this case, selecting two words is perfectly fine. What would not be ok for your hourglass would be something like 'Time management is a very important skill'.

To be in the text, or not to be in the text.

Another doubt that people usually have is: should I select the keyword from the words the author used, or should I come up with another word?

Again, flexibility is the solution. When you read and understand the paragraph, ask yourself what word would help you trigger the concept (a bit like if you were writing the title of a folder on your laptop). If the word you have thought of is in the text, select it. If it is not, write it on the side.

At times, an example/analogy/image will come to mind when reading and understanding—that can become your keyword. Your mind loves tangible images: they travel the easiest through the neck of the hourglass!

This could be simpler some of you than for others. One of the reasons resides in your cognitive styles. There are people who find it very easy to select a word that will represent a whole concept, while others will tend to lean more towards phrases and sentences. There will be people who when reading an abstract concept will struggle, while others will be able to picture it very clearly. One of the things we do at Genius in 21 Days is to understand the way in which you specifically represent the information you receive, so that we can share with you all the strategies that suit your unique learning profile. Remember: at geniusbychoice.co.uk/gift, you will be able to find a special gift for all our book readers to help you apply every technique mentioned more effectively.

Before moving on to the next paragraph, I suggest you apply the first five steps to a text. If you have already taken the reading tests in Part II, those are a perfect basis for some Low-Stakes practice to begin with. Alternatively, you can practise on the steps one-to-five text that you have just read.

Words: 1,452   Time (in seconds): _____

Hourglass Six: Next paragraph

{Easy Peasy layer}

After selecting your label, keywords and details, you can continue with the work paragraph by paragraph. There will be paragraphs that you will not need, others in which you will only select a label and some details, others in which you will not find any relevant detail but only concepts. Be flexible!

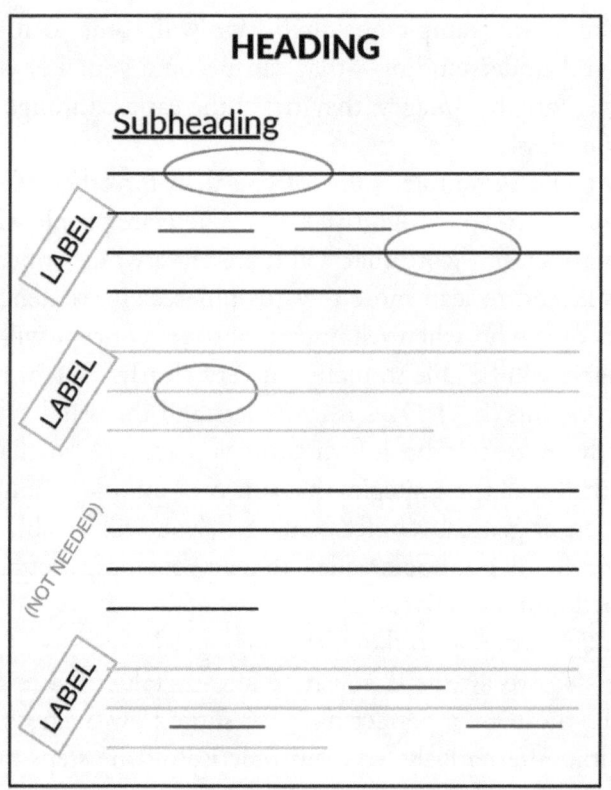

Words: 52   Time (in seconds): _____

Hourglass Seven: Check and skim (after one hour of study)

{Easy Peasy layer}

Re-read only labels, keywords and details to make sure they are enough to recall all the concepts you need, and that none of them are redundant. If you have understood the concepts, very often you will realise you have selected more words than necessary; in that case, remove the ones you do not need: the simpler, the better.

PRO HACK

Once you master the first seven steps, you can dabble in an alternative strategy (called Pro Processing), which will make you even faster.

This needs to be combined with the Strategic Reading Techniques, so if you have not read that part yet, I would suggest you do so first (Part Two—Reading).

In the Pro Processing strategy, the first steps are the same: you will need to read and understand a paragraph and select a label for it. However, after finding your label for the paragraph, you move on to the next paragraph—instead of digging deeper to see if there are any more details and concepts for which to find a keyword. For next paragraph you once more find your label and move again to the next one; and so on, paragraph by paragraph, until the end of the chapter.

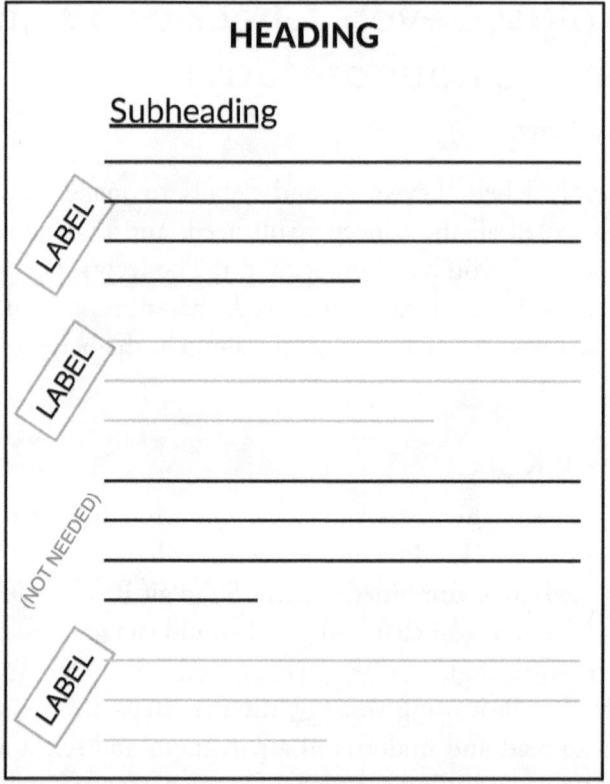

At this point, go back to each paragraph and, looking at the label you have written on the side, try to recall the concepts inside the paragraph. Only then—and only if needed—add some keywords and details for the concepts you have missed while recalling.

The advantage of this strategy is that, by going back to the different paragraphs on a second occasion, the number of keywords selected will decrease significantly. This happens for two reasons:

Number one is that labelling each paragraph first allows you to have a global idea of what is covered, so that you can select the concepts to translate into keywords in a targeted way. When you do not use this strategy, what may happen is that you also end up selecting keywords for some concepts that are ultimately, in the global context, not relevant.

The second reason why this strategy will decrease the number of your keywords is that you will realise how, having already understood and processed the concepts, you need far fewer words than you would have originally instinctively selected.

PRO HACK

Here we have spoken about codes such as writing the label alongside the text, circling the keywords and underlining the details. There are several codes that you can use in a text to help you with the internalisation and processing of the concepts, and they are all very subjective. There are people who love numbering lists or using special colours or symbols for some specific kinds of information. Have fun and enjoy it—this will help the process!

Words: 461   *Time (in seconds):* _____

CHAPTER THIRTEEN

Organising

[Desk is better]

Hourglass Eight: Mind Maps

{Easy Peasy layer}

Now that you have processed the information, it is time to organise it. This is so your mind can remember it better and spot connections and links that may have gone unnoticed due to the linear nature of the text. What you need is a note-taking technique; one that allows you to connect information, be able to move from global vision to details, have multiple pages on one sheet of paper, express your cognitive styles freely, think easily, find information in an instant, remember everything fast, be able to manipulate the information by adding things where they belong, and—why not—have fun.

Sounds impossible to create? A bit. But someone succeeded in this Herculean task: it was the late Tony Buzan, an English author and educational consultant.

Observing the way some geniuses of the past used to take notes, which was mostly through keywords and graphic representations of the concepts, and putting this together with the latest studies that had been carried out on how the brain works, Buzan created mind maps.

Mind maps allow you to do all that I mentioned, and even more.

Zoom In—Zoom Out

I always compare mind maps to a helicopter. Have you ever been on one? (No worries if you have not, the example works regardless!)

Imagine that you jump into a helicopter. In that moment the helicopter is on the ground, and you are able to notice all the details of the environment around you. As the helicopter rises not the air, what happens? Your perspective changes. You see fewer close details, but you start noticing the geography of the city. You can see where there is a park and where there are factories, the urban centre and the parks. You can see the main streets that connect different areas and the river that runs across it, dividing and unifying at once.

When you learn or try to express your ideas, have you ever had the feeling that you know the details yet it is hard for you to zoom out and see the global picture? Or that you know how things are connected but some important details slip your mind. Well, mind maps will be your helicopter to move from the ground to the sky and back: from the details to the global vision, to the details again.

Mind maps will become your best ally when organising any kind of information, because they will be your tool to zoom in and out at your pleasure.

However, there is a 'but'.

Why Mind Maps never worked on you

Tony Buzan had for sure a genius mind himself, and mind maps are one of the greatest learning inventions ever brought to life. However, there is something you need to know.

We often run taster sessions for our Genius in 21 Days programme, and when we start talking about mind maps the Mentor leading the session will ask: 'Who amongst you has ever heard of mind maps?' A lot of people raise their hands. 'Who amongst you applies them on a daily basis?' A lot of hands go down. It may be that, if you were attending one of our taster sessions, you would do the exact same thing.

When I witnessed this for the first time I was really surprised. It was during the initial taster sessions we ran in London. I had just come from Italy where I had trained and worked, and where, in response to the same question, people would usually answer that they had never heard of mind maps. In London, though, I could see that most people had heard of them, but there was just a small proportion who would use them.

I was puzzled, because for me mind maps are a tool I use on an almost daily basis to organise any information: what I need to do that day, projects I have in mind, training sessions I am preparing, books I am studying, meetings I am running, ideas I want to brainstorm, notes I am taking, and so on. How could people *know about* them but not *use* them?

Then I remembered that when I was in middle school, preparing for my final exam, my dad had introduced me to mind maps to help me keep up with everything I had to learn. The idea sounded interesting, so I had tried to apply them, but after a couple of days they seemed more time-consuming than my previous method, and the advantage they brought did not seem to be worth the effort. Only years later, when at eighteen I took the old version of what is now the Genius in 21 Days course, did I realise that mind maps do not have to be time-consuming, and that they can in fact help you to save so much time, while also becoming a bridge between the written language and the way your mind thinks.

As I looked into the reasons behind why all these people were not exploiting the full power of mind maps, it became apparent that, although most of them had learnt about mind maps at school or university, there were two problems at play.

Most people had learnt how to apply them only for a specific purpose, such as putting down some ideas, and were not aware of all the other areas in which mind maps can really be of benefit.

But the most important problem was that everyone who was not applying them had not been taught how to use them effectively, in terms of their way of learning and the purpose of the map.

Remember—everyone has a different cognitive profile (no, I have not got tired of repeating it yet!), which impacts not only the way you understand and process information, but also how you organise and express it. When creating a mind map, this becomes even more evident. Mind maps can easily adapt to any cognitive profile, but if you do not know how to do so then you may just find them ineffective because they do not reflect *your* way of learning.

Once you understand how *you* should use them, you will definitely be surprised by how powerful they are and how they will be able to make your life so much easier.

How to create a Mind Map

Ready. Steady.

Let's start with the material you need to create a mind map. Make sure you have the following items on your desk: paper sheets, a pen and some colours; or, if you prefer being more technological, your tablet. Disclaimer: colours are preferable but not mandatory, especially for those quick maps that you do on the go. However, if you are able to have a few at hand, you will appreciate it.

It is strongly recommended you use plain sheets of paper: to allow your mind to be free to use the space however it prefers. If you need to choose between drawing a mind map on ruled paper or not drawing a mind map at all, then ruled paper will do just fine.

Now we will go through all the steps that you need to take. If you have some paper with you, I suggest you reproduce each step as you read it.

Before we go on, I want you to keep one thing in mind. The rules that you will find in the different steps are not real 'rules', but rather 'suggestions' that will allow you to get started and create effective maps in the simplest way possible. However, one of the great advantages of mind mapping is that it allows you to be flexible, following the flow of your thoughts and playing with the concepts and the space. Initially, the best thing to do is to follow these guidelines, but as you create more maps you will see that your style will start to present itself.

Go.

The first thing to start with is the centre, in which you will place the main idea. Make sure it is as central as possible, as to give you balanced space all on all sides. You can draw an image that represents the main idea or write the title of what the mind map will be about. When I am taking notes and I am not sure about what the topic will be, I usually draw an empty circle that I will fill in later. Be flexible!

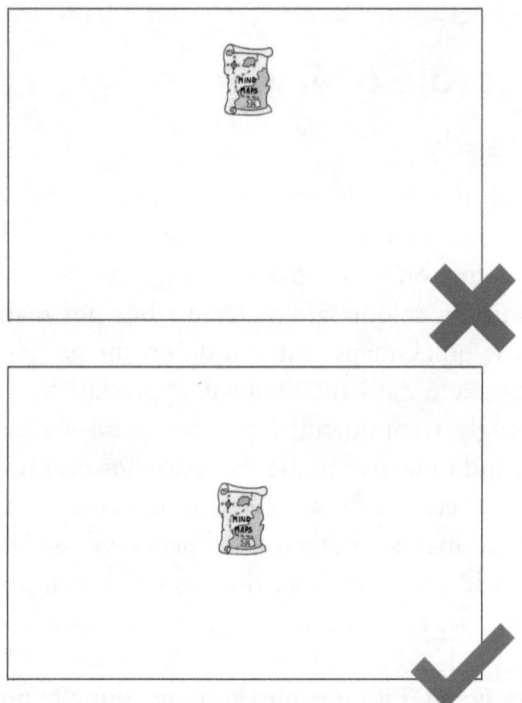

Branches

After the centre, it is time to start drawing the branches. Imagine the paper to be a clock: the first branch will be at one o'clock and from there you will move on clockwise.

You will have different layers of branches: main ones that will start from the centre, secondary ones that will start from the end of the main ones, and so forth.

To keep the map as clear as possible, always make sure that the next layer starts from the end of the previous one and moves towards the exterior. You could compare mind maps to onions. If you slice an onion into two halves and you look at it from above, it gives a clear idea of the different layers. In the same way, by looking at your mind map it should be easy to understand the separate layers it is made from.

The branches are curved, as your mind will be more receptive to them this way and it will be easier for you to manage space with curved branches.

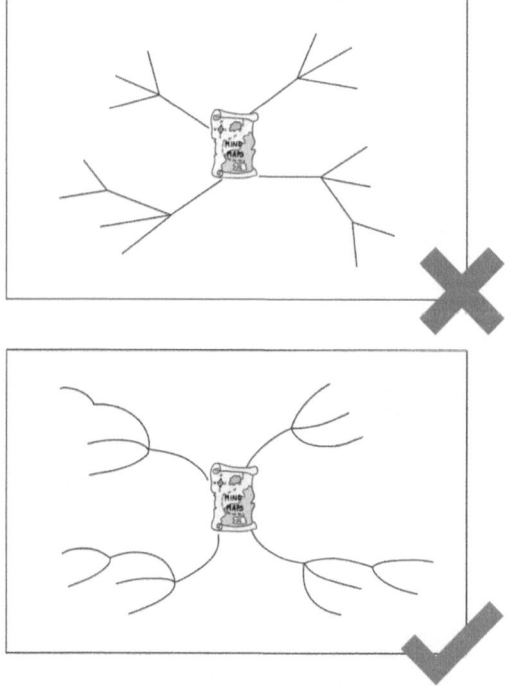

You will write the words on top of each branch, not at the end of them. Again, this will make your map clearer. For the same reason, get used to writing in block capitals, as this will help you to read what you are writing easily. When you have two words, you can also choose to write one on top and one underneath the branch.

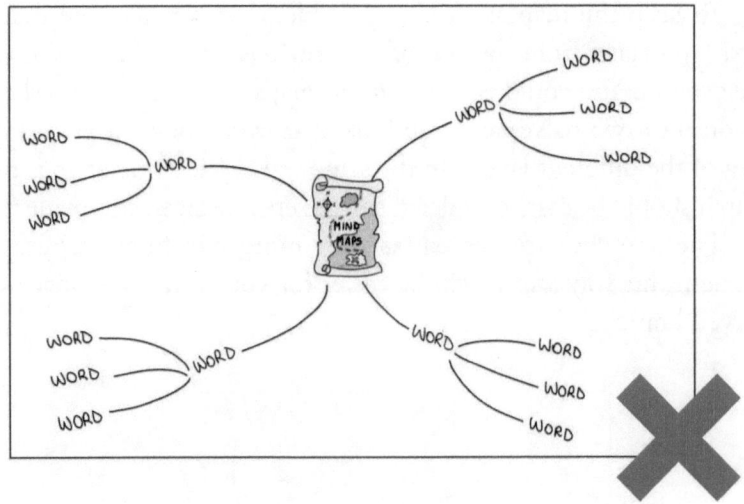

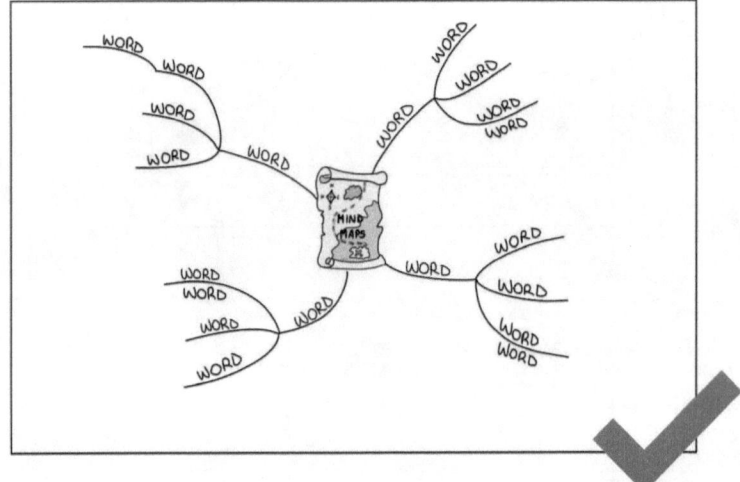

As you become more experienced, you will learn how to manage the length of the branches according to the content of the map. At the beginning, make sure you do not make your written branches too long, else you will soon run out of space. As a general rule, each branch should be as long as the word on top of it.

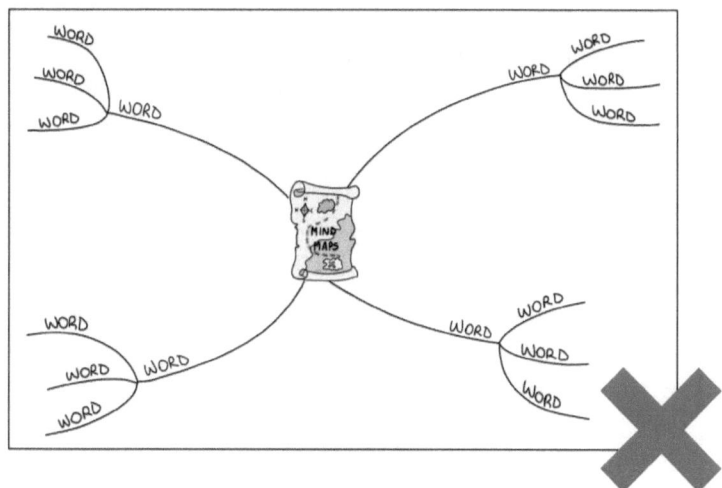

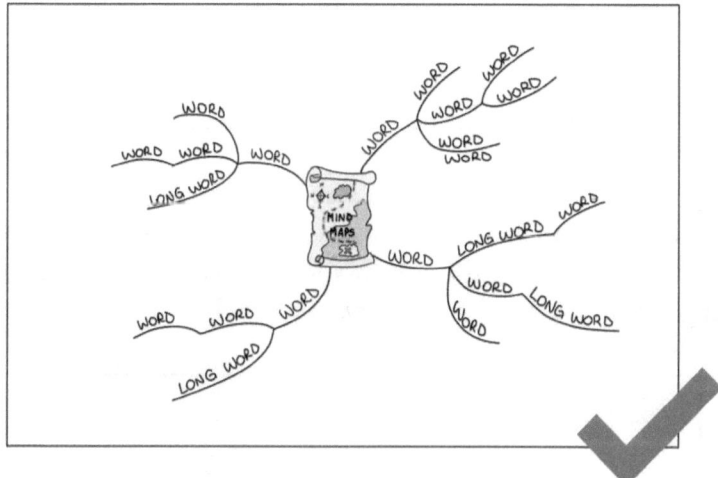

Contents of the Mind Map

On the branches you will need to insert single words or groups of two to three words. Never write sentences, as that will annihilate most of the advantages of using a mind map.

On each layer of the map you will be inserting a different hierarchical level of information, from more general to more specific.

If you are creating your mind map out of a text, the centre may be the heading of your chapter, while on the main branches you could have subheadings, on secondary branches labels, and then beyond those keywords and details (see Chapter Eleven—Decoding and Understanding).

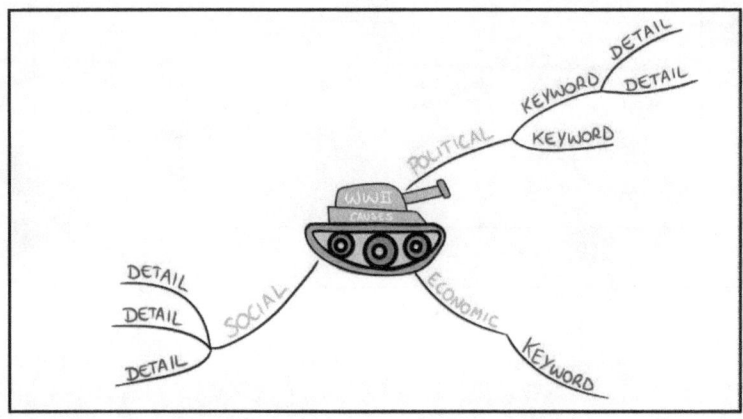

If you are creating your daily to-do map, the centre may be the date, the main branches the categories of things you need to do (calls, emails, personal errands, health) and the secondary branches everything that falls into each category.

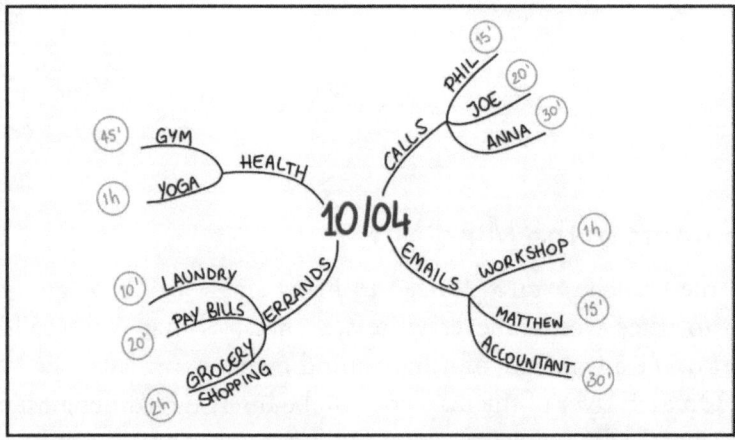

Visuals

Visuals are an incredibly powerful tool to use on a mind map. The reason they are so powerful is because our memory is mostly visual, and so by drawing an image it will become much easier to remember things.

At times people ask me: 'Do I need to draw visuals on top of all the words?' You do not have to, as flexibility is what matters. If you feel inspired to and you have time, you can draw them on each branch, but if you are in a rush there may be times in which you do not draw any.

On an average map that you need to remember, I would suggest placing visuals on all the main branches and next to words that are hard to remember.

When we get to talking about visuals, some people think 'I am not an artist, I am not good at drawing'. Well, you do not need to be an artist to create visuals on a mind map. They need to be effective for you—and the first thing that comes to your mind when you think of that idea is perfectly fine!

When you look at a word, you will usually be able to think of an image to represent it (if you struggle with this, go to Part IV—Memorise). In general, there are two different strategies you can use: thinking about the meaning of the word and thinking about its sound.

Here is a simple example. For the word 'horizontal', you could draw someone lying down (based on the meaning) or a horizon (based on the sound). Both ways are fine, just use the very first thing that comes to your mind.

Meaning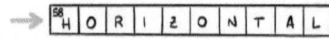

Sound

My friend John

Distinctive features:
He has freckles and wears glasses

My friend Sarah

Distinctive features:
She has curly hair and a red car

As I mentioned, visuals are not mandatory and if you really do not feel like trying them out I will not push you. However, once you start using them, you will realise that visuals are a game changer in a number of situations.

In the revision phase, they make the process of revision faster and more fun. Let's do a quick exercise. Within the following map, look for the words 'easy review'.

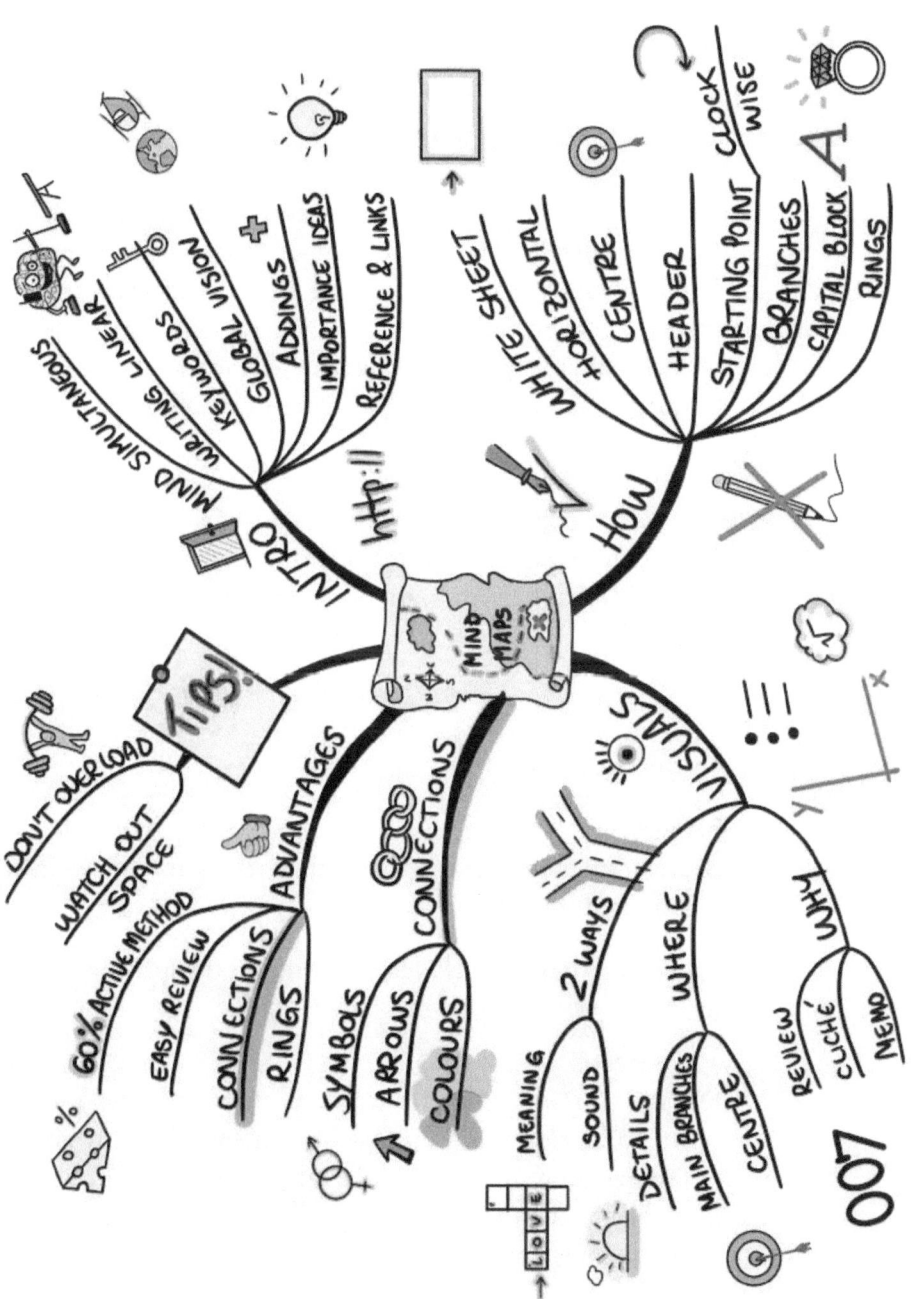

Now, in the same map, look for the image of the pencil with a red cross. Which one was easier to find? The pencil of course. The reason for this is that all words are made up of the same twenty-six characters, while images can play with different shapes and colours, which makes them unique and more easily recognisable.

Visuals will also help you remember the content of the map in a much simpler way, almost effortlessly. Whenever I have a map containing some precise details I need to remember (lists, specific words and so on), by drawing a visual next to them I often do not even need to apply any memorisation technique.

Not to mention that using colours, images and arrows makes the process of learning much more enjoyable than using dull notes. And fun, as we saw, helps you become more effective!

The other reason why colours and visuals will make your life easier is that they are the perfect way to connect concepts to one other. This will help you to compare different theories, analyse differences and see relationships that before would have gone unnoticed.

PRO HACK

I want to give you two more tips:

1. Remember not to overload a mind map. It is preferable to create more than one map rather than trying to squeeze in too much information.

2. Watch out for the space! Make sure you use the space evenly.

PRO HACK

Maps are meant to be clear and personal, so if there are any words that you consider as more important, play around with them. You can make them bigger than the others regardless of their hierarchy, and you can use colours to highlight them. It is your map—allow yourself to be creative.

> **PRO HACK**

Clichés: it can happen that the same keywords or details need to be repeated across mind maps. In such instances you can create clichés: fixed images that you will use consistently, to represent the same concept and make the process faster.

Where you can apply Mind Maps

Once you start using mind maps, you will see that they have an almost infinite number of applications. Any time you have concepts to organise, they will be your life raft.

- Note-taking
- Summarising books, documents, paperwork
- Planning (a holiday, your day/week/month/year)
- Goal-setting
- Learning languages, since they are extremely helpful in organising the grammar rules of any language
- Organising information
- Making decisions
- Brainstorming ideas
- Preparing a presentation
- Planning a project

And these are but a few examples!

What I would suggest is that you do one per day, working through the range of different applications. Be organised: if you are doing them on a tablet, organise them in folders; if you are using a pen and paper, keep them in a binder.

Make sure to use them: try, make mistakes and learn from them! There is no such thing as a perfect mind map, but mind maps can work perfectly for you as long as you decide to use their true potential.

If you need to memorise the contents of your map, Chapter Fourteen—Characteristics of Your Memory and Chapter Fifteen—Velcro Technique will help you immensely.

Words: 2,746   *Time (in seconds):* _____

Inspiration Time from Our Genius Alumni

What can I say, Genius in 21 Days has unlocked potentials that I knew existed in my mind but didn't know how to unlock and use it.

I took the course because I wanted proven techniques that would enable me to increase my reading speed and at the same time retain the information I consumed.

The initial assessment I took to determine my learning style gave me a very valuable insight, allowing me to understand where I needed to focus on to get the best results in an efficient manner.

After taking the course, my speed reading has doubled and I have now a better ability to recall the information I consumed as a result of the techniques I've learned.

The entire course was presented in a relaxed and fun atmosphere which made the learning process easy to follow and understand.

I highly recommend to take the Genius in 21 Days course, as you will get in return more than what you expected. To put it simply, it's life-changing: the course puts you back in charge of your mind and enables you to utilise it in an efficient manner no matter how complicated whatever you want to learn may seem at the start.

It will have you fall in love with learning again and you will come out of the course finding your own inner self that was once curious about the world and eager to learn it all. That's my experience.

The entire team, with their infectious enthusiasm and energy to see me succeed, has kindled my passion for learning and I am forever grateful for Genius in 21 Days, for they have shown me how to unlock my own potential.

Joey Kifle - Business Manager

PART IV.
MEMORISE

Think for a moment about how many hours in your life you have spent reading books; how much information you have tried to take in, repeating out loud, re-reading and re-writing.

If every piece of information were a brick, and you had to pile up all these bricks, how big would the tower be? It would be incredibly tall and impressive, would it not? That tower represents your fortress, the starting point from which to build all the results you want to achieve, because as Julian Barnes said, 'The more you learn, the less you fear'.

Now, from that tower, remove all the bricks that represent all the information that you no longer remember. Oops! What just happened to your fortress? It probably no longer looks so vast and stable.

Unfortunately, this is what years spent applying the wrong methods will have created: a hollow fortress.

Now imagine if you could learn anything extremely fast; if you could have fun while learning it, and could remember it forever when needed. How many more bricks would you have in your fortress?

It may sound like an impossible dream, but it is actually something our brain is designed to be able to do.

From surviving to evolving; from creating new ideas to solving problems; from looking back to the events in our life to imagining future scenarios—memory is something we have always needed, since the very beginning of time. We have been programmed to use it properly. It is just a matter of knowing how to harness the incredible power of our brain.

So let's start our journey. We are going to find out what the characteristics of our memory are, how to put them together in the Velcro Technique, and how to apply the Velcro Technique to different pieces of information. Finally, we will talk about how to commit information to our long-term memory.

Words: 317   Time (in seconds): _____

CHAPTER FOURTEEN

Characteristics

[Bed is fine]
{No Effort layer}

So, what are those characteristics that will allow you to immediately remember things faster?

Firstly, your memory is mostly visual, which means images are easier to retain than abstract information. If I say to you 'royalty', what comes immediately to mind: the writing or the image? Most people will answer 'the image'. Which particular image will depend on the association each individual has made with 'royalty': for someone it may be Queen Elizabeth II; for someone else it could be a crown; for someone else the book from which they receive royalties every month; and for someone else, something else.

The same process applies with names. Have you ever met someone in the street and thought: 'I know I've seen this person somewhere, but what is their name?' This happens because a face is an image, so it is easier for it to stick in your memory. Names are abstract information, so most of the time they go straight in one ear and out the other.

How can you use this? When you need to remember a detail, picture it vividly in your mind as an image to make sure it becomes more memorable.

PRO HACK

What can you do when the detail is not an object but an abstract word? There are three options.

Number one is to use the first thing that comes to mind when you think about that concept. For most abstract concepts, your mind already has an image, and most of the time this image will be enough.

When it is very hard for you to find an image related to the concept, you can look for a tangible word with a similar sound to the abstract word, so that your mind can picture something and, from that sound, come up with the word.

A third way, which I find myself using pretty often, is to mix the two: finding an image that reminds you of the concept and adding a little detail that will trigger the exact word you have to use. This is the path I take when I need to be particularly precise in the term I use, because the detail for the sound allows me to be very specific.

Secondly, your memory is associative, so it works like a chain. Once you pull the first ring, all the others follow. Proust ate a madeleine and his mind set off on a journey; you hear a song and your mind suddenly remembers a particular moment; you smell a scent and you start reminiscing about an important person in your life.

So, when you need to memorise something new, link it to something that you already know, and you will notice how much longer you will be able to retain it for.

Thirdly, your memory is emotion-based. When a strong emotion is involved, it is much easier to remember anything. Your mind finds it particularly easy to recall something that you find funny, sexy, disgusting or scary. If you can make the information 'emotional', then you will remember it!

Fourthly, remembering places comes naturally to most people. When you picture an object in a specific place—rather than picturing it without context—it will be easier to recall.

Words: 536   Time (in seconds): _____

CHAPTER FIFTEEN

The Velcro Technique

[Bed is fine]

It is great to know the characteristics of your memory, but how can you put them together to start remembering anything quickly and effectively?

To understand how to do it, you need to think about Velcro. Velcro is the common name of hook-and-loop fasteners, taken from the brand they were first distributed by. How does Velcro work? And why can it help you to memorise things better?

Hook-and-loop fasteners are made to stick together two strips. In order to do so, they are made of two main sides: on one side there are many tiny hooks, on the other side there are a lot of loops. When you press the two sides together, the hooks catch the loops and the strips 'stick' together. The more hooks and loops you have, the more bound the strips will be.

'Giulia, how can this help me to remember things?' Time to reveal this powerful technique…

There are five steps to follow, and thinking about Velcro will help you to master this technique.

1. Trigger (aka one of the two strips)
2. New Information (aka the other strip)
3. PAV (aka hooks and loops)
4. Lock (aka pressing the two strips)
5. Visualise (aka looking at the strips that have been pressed and admiring your work)

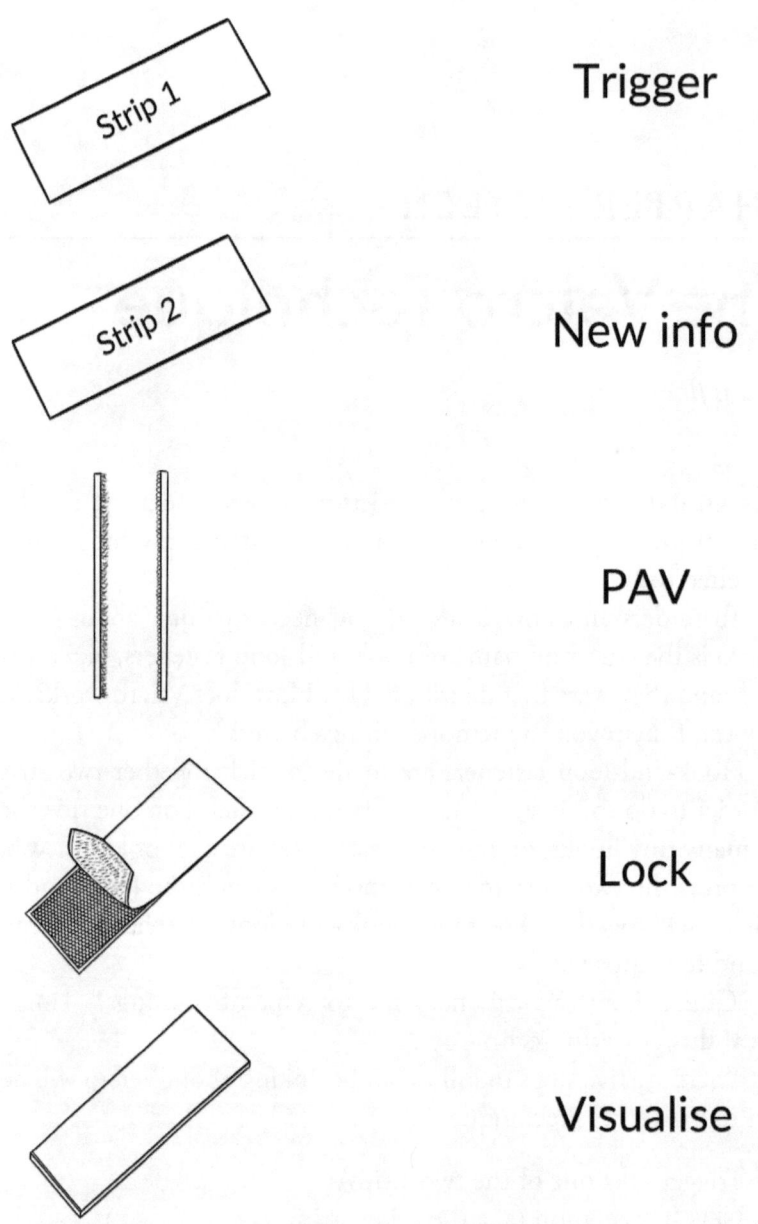

Let us now work through these steps, one by one.

Words: 221   *Time (in seconds):* _____

Velcro One: Trigger

{Easy Peasy layer}

Remember when we said that your memory works by associating your new information to something you already know? Well, this step is where you identify what you already know.

What happens when you skip this step?

Skipping this step means you take in pieces of information, only to then find that all these pieces are 'floating' inside your brain, not knowing where they belong. It is like trying to memorise a formula but not looking at the entire equation, only what is on the other side of the '='. It means knowing a lot of words in a foreign language without knowing what they mean. It is really not worth the effort.

How does this step work

Your Trigger can be one of two things: what is already part of your knowledge, or the question you will ask yourself to trigger what you have learned.

Imagine you want to learn that bear in Italian is 'orso'. Your Trigger will be 'bear', which is what you already know.

Or you could be learning a historical date you knew nothing about before, for example that in 1905 Las Vegas was founded. In this case, you need to ask yourself: 'What do I want to remember: that Las Vegas was founded in 1905? Or that one of the events that happened in 1905 was that Las Vegas was founded?' The difference is tiny but distinct. At times it does not really matter, and in those cases you can select either piece as a trigger. In other cases, you know clearly what the trigger must be.

What do you need to do with your Trigger? Simply ask yourself: what is the first image that comes to mind for this trigger? When you think about a bear, what is the first thing that comes to mind? Picture it in your mind vividly. For some people it will be a grizzly bear, for others it will be Winnie the Pooh, for others a polar bear. When you think about Las Vegas, what is the first thing that comes to mind? Maybe it is casinos, or the Bellagio fountains, or lights, or roulette. As long as it is a tangible image and it reminds you of your Trigger, it is perfect. Or if you selected 1905 as your Trigger, what could be an image for the five? Maybe you think about a high five, or a fiver. As long as it is a tangible image, it is perfect.

This is not a step you should overthink. You have one simple thing to do, which is to ask: what is the first image that comes to mind? Your brain has already created so many associations throughout your life, and you just need to go with whichever one presents itself first.

Mistakes you want to avoid

There are two mistakes that people make when picturing their Trigger.

The first is that they look at the new information and select a trigger that 'fits' with the new information. This is a mistake because, when you see that the new information could be a characteristic of the Trigger, you may be tempted to adjust the trigger so that it fits that characteristic. This is a problem, because the strength of the trigger comes from its irremovability, its steadiness. The trigger is a pillar for you, it is the image your mind automatically goes to when you think about that word. Do not change it in favour of the new information. When your mind will be thinking about the trigger, the first thing that will come to mind will be the image you had originally thought about (not the changed one), so it will not find what it is looking for and will not be able to recall the information.

PRO HACK Double Trigger

There are some situations in which what you need is a double trigger, and not keeping this in mind may create serious difficulty in retaining the correct information you need. This happens especially when you have very complex information to memorise, such as the verb conjugations in a foreign language, or when you have a series of common categories associated to an item and with details to follow.

To explain, I will give a simple example. Imagine I have a potential client and I would like to remember his passions; his reasons to buy my product; and some information about his business, such as the name, number of employees and vision for his future. If, as a trigger, you just used the name of the client, you would find yourself with a very long sequence of information to memorise. Using the double trigger hack, you will have shorter sequences to learn and you will be able to access the information quicker when required.

All you need to do is to create an image that includes both the potential client and the kind of information you want to associate to him. The image you use for the potential client will always be the same, but it will be associated with different images every time (passions, reasons to buy, business). You will find yourself with a series of triggers, all different from each other, so you will not get confused and will be able to access the information quickly and effectively.

This is an example, but you will see that this hack will find many applications, every time you want to be faster and not get confused.

Words: 906   Time (in seconds): _____

Velcro Two: New Information
{Easy Peasy layer}

This is the king of your five-step process. It is the information that you want to commit to memory and (in most cases) never forget.

What happens when you skip this step

The New Information is the king, so it is very unlikely that you will skip it. However, what may happen is that you focus so much on the other steps that you forget to follow this step properly, so read carefully what this step entails.

How does this step work

Your memory is visual, and so your New Information must be too. During this step you have to find an image to represent your New Information, as explained when discussing the characteristics of your memory.

> *Eg* if the new information is orso, you could think of horse, torso, ...

When the New Information is very complex and there is no one image that on its own can represent the full information, what you can do is to split the word and find separate images. Each image will become the trigger for the following one.

> *Eg* scarpa can be split into scar and pa. Scar can be represented by a scar, and pa can be your dad or your grandpa.

Mistakes you want to avoid

The main mistake people make when finding an image for their New Information is to underestimate the power of their own brain. They do this by overcomplicating the image they select, out of fear of not remembering every detail otherwise. You need to find the balance between being over-simplistic and being over-precise. Being over-simplistic will lead you to forget the information; being over-precise will see you waste precious time.

> *Eg* DO NOT DO: I have selected the image of a horse for orso, but they don't sound exactly the same, so I need to add a detail to remove the h and a detail to add an 'o' at the end... Nor, torso has an extra T, so I can imagine some tea being wiped away from my torso.

What I usually suggest is that you find one or two main images without minding the small details. If after one hour you still remember those small details that you did not actively memorise, wonderful. If you do not, that is the cue to add them. Always adding them from the beginning will risk wasting time, because very often they are not needed. Checking after one hour, however, gives you the peace of mind that you want, because you will know that if you do not remember those details you still have time to add them.

Words: 435   Time (in seconds): _____

Velcro Three: PAV
{Easy Peasy layer}

Now that you have found your images, it is time to lay down those hooks and loops that will allow them to stick together.

PAV is an acronym that stands for Paradox, Action and Vividness: the three ingredients that will become the glue between your Trigger and New Information.

When we described the Velcro, we said that the more hooks and loops there are, the more the strips will stick to each other. So, let's see how we can have as many hooks and loops as possible.

What happens when you skip this step

Skipping this step leads to one simple but terrible consequence: you will remember about ten per cent of what you have tried to commit to memory (and I am being generous in my estimation here). Imagine the two strips, without hooks and loops. How can they stick together?

How does this step work

This is the step where you make the Trigger interact with the New Information (in this order), by creating an action between the two.

This action needs to be the first one that comes to mind, but you will make it more memorable by applying some PAV.

> *Eg* Our bear is riding a horse

Paradox

The key question you need to ask yourself is: 'If I saw this in a crowd, would I notice it?' If it is dull and boring, you will not retain it. Remember that our memory is based on emotions, so there needs to be something weird in the interaction between the two images in order for you to notice it amid the ocean of information you are subjected to every day.

Action

Make sure there is an action going on between the Trigger and the New Information, and not just some static image that includes both. Movement wins over stillness.

Vividness

When you picture the images, ask yourself to see them clearly, in as much detail as you can. The more of the five senses you can include, the more vivid it will be: this is because you will be laying down more hooks and loops on your Velcro.

Mistakes you want to avoid

The first mistake you may make is that you could be tempted to apply PAV to the wrong phase. PAV is the glue between the strips, it is not the Trigger. At times people, after selecting their trigger, enrich it with weird details to make it memorable. Use PAV to make the action and New Information more memorable, not to change your Trigger, to which you need to do nothing other than keep the first image that came to mind.

The second mistake you may make is when, by looking at the Trigger, you notice it has something in common with the New

Information and so you decide that you 'will remember it' and therefore do not create an association. Let me tell you something. If you do it once, at a time when you are not memorising much, this could work. But when you are memorising many pieces of information, this will become a problem, as you will not be able to easily recall any association.

> *Eg* DO NOT DO: Ball - Palla. well, I always play ball with my pals, so I will not need to associate it, I will remember it

The third mistake happens when you do not respect the order of the steps, but instead begin your interaction at the New Information and then move to the Trigger. I know that at times there are some associations that just work perfectly in the opposite direction, so as an exception you can do it, but only when your association is so perfect that you feel it is worthy of a creativity award. If it becomes the rule, your mind will start getting very confused.

> *Eg* bear - orso. A horse kicks a bear

PRO HACK

There are four main emotions that our mind remembers extremely easily. When your PAV association is either funny, disgusting, violent or sexy, you are very likely to remember it. So, at the end of creating a PAV association, use those four emotions as a checklist and ask yourself: was it funny, disgusting, violent or sexy? If the answer is yes to one of these, you are on the right track! If the answer is no for all of them, it is just a matter of making it more so.

Words: 732   Time (in seconds): _____

Velcro Four: Lock

{Easy Peasy layer}

This is the step where you will make sure that your two strips stick together by pressing them against each other. It is very quick to complete, and you will become addicted to it once you see the difference it makes in how effectively you remember your information.

What happens when you skip this step

Not locking your association carries with it one big risk: that you may not picture the last image vividly enough, and therefore may forget it or get it confused with a similar image.

How does this step work

In order to lock your PAV association, you need to add a final detail to the story to fix the right image in your mind. This is usually an action that is typical of the image you have selected. Ask yourself: what can this image do that makes it recognisable? If it is a cat, it could scratch; if it is a dog, it could play or lick; if it is a chair, someone could sit on it. And so on.

Mistakes you want to avoid

Adding a locking detail does not mean adding extra images to your association. You do not want to complicate things—because the simpler, the faster. The purpose of the locking action is to engrave the last image in your mind, as you could overlook it otherwise; the purpose is not to add more objects to the story.

> *Eg* If the last image is a cat, the locking detail could be an action like scratching or meowing; DO NOT DO: using a ball of yarn or chasing a bird

Words: 267 *Time (in seconds):* _____

Velcro Five: Visualise
{Easy Peasy layer}

Your memory is visual, and this is the step where you make sure you harness all the power of your visual memory. In his book *Psycho-Cybernetics*, Maxwell Maltz said: 'The mind cannot tell the difference between an actual experience and one vividly imagined.' An easy example to demonstrate how true this can be is dreams. Imagine you are dreaming that you are in a forest. It is night-time, there is a nice breeze and you can see the moon through the branches of the trees. At a certain point, you hear some steps. And a howl. You start walking faster, but the steps are getting closer. So you begin running as fast as you can, but you can hear them getting closer and closer. You keep running, and you stumble on the big root of a tree. You fall down, and when you turn around the wolf is jumping at you.

You wake up. Are you relaxed and serene? No: you will probably be nervous; you may be sweaty; your heart may be beating faster. You may even check under the bed to make sure the wolf is not hiding there. Your body will be showing the same symptoms that it would show if you were in real danger, even though it was just a dream.

This happens because you imagine it so vividly that, to your mind, it is real.

You may be asking yourself: 'What does this have to do with memory?' Well, we are getting there.

What is easier for you to remember: an actual experience, or something that you read in a book? The former. Therefore, accessing the power of your imagination to vividly picture what you are learning will help you remember things better.

What happens when you skip this step

Skipping this step leads to one simple word: disaster. It is like baking the most amazing cake and letting it fall to the floor before eating it.

It is like taking a masterpiece and throwing it into the bin. Do not skip it.

How does this step work

All you need to do is to picture the association you have created. Initially I would suggest closing your eyes to do it, as it will help you to focus on picturing it clearly. As you become more accustomed to doing it, you will not have to close your eyes all the time, because you will have developed your ability to picture images with your eyes open.

Mistakes you want to avoid

There is only one real mistakes you can make in this step: spending too long on it. Your mind actually has already visualised the whole association; this phase is only meant to last a couple of seconds, as you will not need more than this to make sure your mind has pictured the association.

Before moving on, let's recap the five steps:

Velcro One: Trigger—Come up with an image for the thing that you already know
Velcro Two: New Information—Come up with an image for the thing that you do not know yet
Velcro Three: PAV—Associate them together with Paradox, Action, Vividness
Velcro Four: Lock—Add a final action to focus your attention on the last image
Velcro Five: Visualise—Close your eyes for a couple of seconds and visualise

Words: 551   *Time (in seconds):* _____

CHAPTER SIXTEEN

Memory Palace—and Its Many Aliases

[Desk is better]

You may have heard of this technique, as it is one of the most publicised. However, knowing that it exists and being able to apply it effectively are two different things, and this becomes even more evident with the Memory Palace (aka Method of loci, Roman Room, Journey Method, Mind Palace). In brief terms, the Memory Palace consists of selecting a place that you know very well (your home for example) and placing each item you need to remember inside that place (thus associating it with that place's objects) in a specific order. But let's first understand why it should work on everyone, why it often does not and how to make sure that it does; because—if you grasp this technique—there are many occasions where you will not want to use any other.

Why It Should Work
{No effort layer}

If I asked you to imagine your kitchen, you would probably be able to recall it with a high level of detail. You would know where the main appliances live, and also where smaller objects are kept. This is because as human beings we have had to develop the ability to recognise and remember places. This makes the Memory Palace a great tool in your arsenal—if you use it well.

Memory Palace is in fact the oldest recorded memory technique. Cicero described the technique In his *De Oratore* some 2,000 years ago: telling the story of Simonides of Ceos, who lived in the fifth century BC. Apparently, Simonides had been hired as a poet for a banquet of nobles. He performed in front of all these people and then he left. Unfortunately, following his departure the building collapsed, killing everyone inside. The bodies were so deformed that it was impossible to recognise who was who, but Simonides had, during his performance, memorised the names of all the guests according to where they were sitting, and so he was able to identify the bodies.

Whether this is history or legend, the fact that the Memory Palace has been around for millennia is a testament to its validity.

Every time you have to remember a long list of items—whether it is what you want to say during a presentation, or the steps you need to follow for a specific procedure, or what someone is telling you—the Memory Palace will be your quick choice. It can also be a great way to memorise Mind Maps (see Chapter Thirteen—passage on Mind Maps).

The reason why it is so effective (and the favourite technique of most memory champions) is that places are easy to remember, and placing images inside a space that you know will make them far more memorable.

Words: 451   Time (in seconds): _____

Why It Does Not Work

{No effort layer}

When I was around fifteen, I was attending a very competitive school in Italy, where every day we were made to study and commit to memory pages and pages of new information. One day, out of desperation, I asked my dad if he could give me some strategies on how to improve my memory. He stood up, and returned a couple of minutes later carrying a book. It was written by a sociologist, and right now I do not even remember the topic of the book. But what I remember very well is that one of the chapters was dedicated to how to improve your memory by using the Method of loci.

I was very excited when I saw it: someone was finally able to make my life easier. I started reading the chapter and did my best to apply what was described in it. I created a journey inside my home; I selected what objects I should use; I tried to memorise a few items in order—but it just seemed so hard, and I gave up. When, years later, I heard about it again and I saw that it was not hard at all, but actually very intuitive and effective, I started exploring why it had not worked on me before.

As I started meeting more and more people who had had a similar experience to mine, I dug deeper, and I came to understand that while the reasons why people had struggled to apply it varied, they were all easy to fix—so that everyone could finally benefit from this powerful technique.

No Velcro

One of the main problems I detected was that the Memory Palace without the Velcro is not enough (Chapter Fifteen—Velcro). With the Velcro Technique we saw how every new piece of information needs to be linked to something that you already know (Trigger). The Memory Palace provides you with innumerable triggers, but if you do not associate the New Information by using the Velcro Technique, you will end up being confused or remembering things vaguely.

Having a list of tidy, effective, easy-to-remember triggers is a huge advantage—one that no other technique supplies as simply—but if you expect that just by having easy triggers and placing the New Information there you will remember things, you are forgetting three out of the five steps;. Of course, it will not be enough.

Panacea

The other problem encountered by most people who do not apply the Memory Palace is that almost everyone expects the Memory Palace to be the panacea for all memory issues. I say 'almost' because I want to leave the benefit of the doubt; but in all my research I have not yet found anyone who clearly defines when the Memory Palace should be applied and when it overcomplicates things.

The Memory Palace has a lot of power, but only if you use it on the right things. Although you may be tempted to use it for everything, there will be some scenarios in which it is not needed, because your Trigger is already there. The Memory Palace works whenever you need a series of triggers to simplify the memorisation. It is much simpler to remember twenty associations between two items than it is one association with twenty items. It is faster; you do not need to worry that if you forget an association everything else will be forgotten; and your triggers are more vivid than if each new information became the trigger for the following one (as happens when you memorise items in a sequence).

However, there are some contexts in which using a Memory Palace would mean overcomplicating things. For example: when you want to learn the vocabulary of a new language (for most languages); when you need to memorise a formula, someone's face and name, historical dates, or numbered lists; and in general any information in which the trigger is already clear (Chapter Eighteen—Applications).

Words: 659 *Time (in seconds):* _____

How It Will Work
{Easy Peasy layer}

How to Start

To make it work immediately, you should start simple. Select one room in your house and picture it in your mind (or you can draw its plan here, below the example, or in your Genius Journal).

Your main topic will be associated either to the door or to the centre of the room. Imagine entering from your door taking a step left and moving clockwise. What are the objects, in order, that you see? Use everything that is stable. For example, if a plant is always in that position you can use it, while you cannot use that book you left on the table yesterday. The reason by now should be pretty clear: your triggers need to be things that are fixed in your memory, as they become your pillars for memorising your new information. Whenever you meet two objects at the same place in the room, for example a cabinet on top of your sink, start from the object at the top and then move down to the bottom. Following this rule will help to you avoid ever creating confusion about the order of the items you are memorising.

Now that you have your triggers, you can start associating and memorising.

Let's do some practice on random words so that you can start seeing how simple it will be.

The main topic is: Exercise.

These are the words you need to memorise in order: ring, leaf, cushion, Colosseum, sponge, butterfly, pharmacy, jewel, carpet, book. They are completely random, just so you can practise, but after practising we are going to see what they could be in real-life application.

GENIUS BY CHOICE

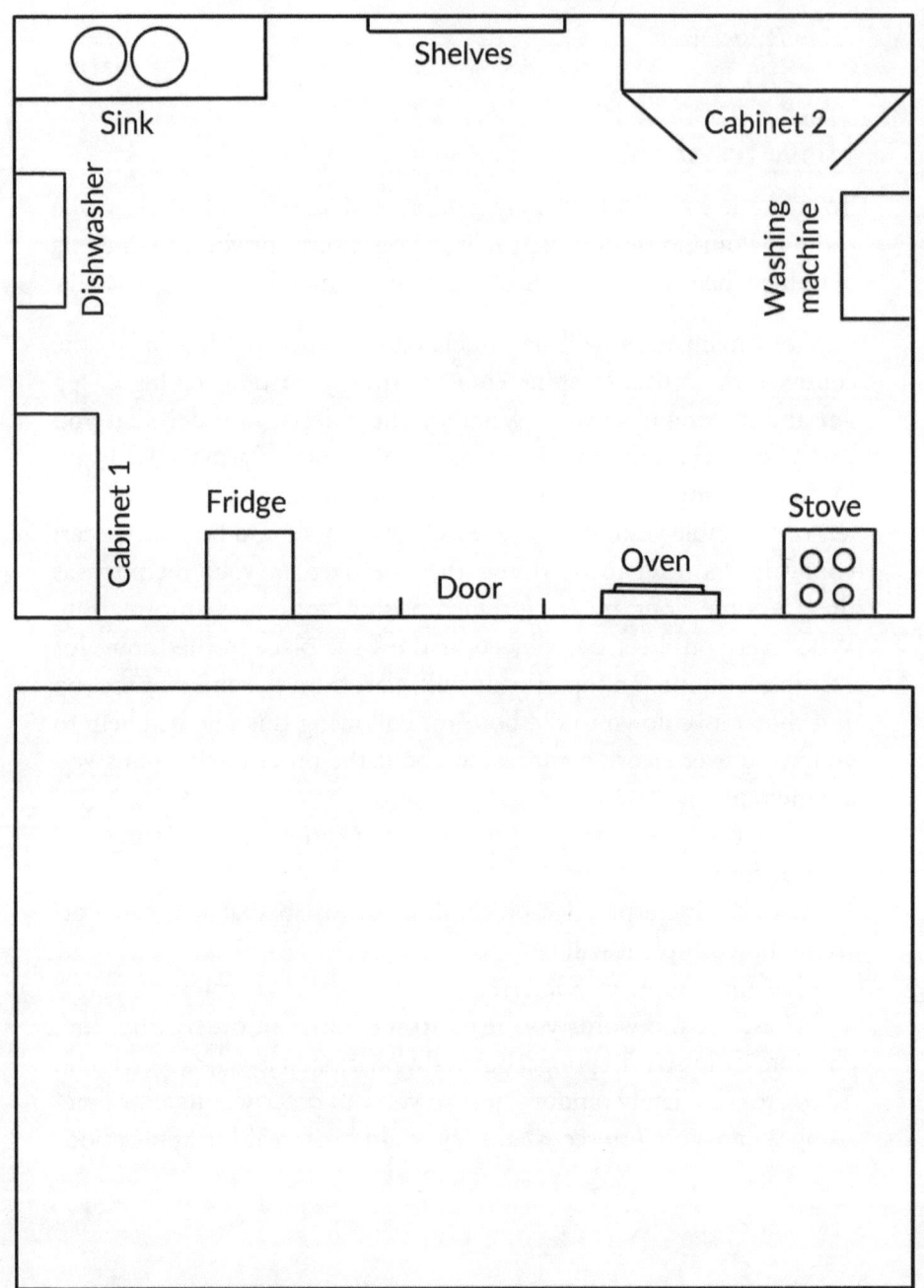

In the drawing above, you can (in order) find: fridge, cabinet, dishwasher, sink, shelves, other cabinet, washing machine, stove, oven.

In your own drawing, select the first ten objects in order. If you have drawn a room with fewer than ten items, there is no problem: once the items end, you can continue your memorisation the next room.

Now, and in order, you will apply the Velcro Technique between each object and the words that you need to memorise. In my case:

Door—exercise
Fridge—ring
Cabinet—leaf
Dishwasher—cushion
Sink—Colosseum
Shelves—sponge
And so on.

Heads up

Mind the triggers

It is important to remember that your trigger this time is not the first fridge that comes to mind (as it would usually be), but it is *the* fridge of the room you have selected, in the place in which your fridge is. The strength of this technique is that it exploits the power of your spatial memory: isolating the triggers from the context or moving them from their place will only create confusion.

I remembered some of it also without Velcro

If you have done the exercise, you will have noticed how quick your recall has been. There will be times in which even just visualising your item next to the object in your room will be enough, however I would not suggest it when you want to remember those pieces of information forever (Chapter Nineteen—Long-Term Memorisation) or if you want to easily utilise the same room more than once (see passage in this chapter—Using the same place y/n). Applying the Velcro

Technique only takes an instant but will allow you to strengthen your retention.

How many objects

Two questions that I am often asked concern how big the objects in the room should be in order to be selected, and how many objects there should be per room.

There is no right or wrong way: flexibility is key (nothing new, eh?). As a rule of thumb, you can select main objects and areas in the room rather than their components (select the bed rather than mattress, sheets, pillow and frame), so that you can apply the Multi-Layer Hack throughout your memorisation.

In terms of the number of objects per room, select as many as you can so that you have multiple triggers at your disposal. If it is a room with just a few objects, no worries. According to what you are memorising, you will either use it for smaller things or in conjunction with other rooms.

I have heard many people who teach the Memory Palace urge their students not to overcrowd a room. This is understandable because, as the Memory Palace is not usually taught in combination with the Velcro Technique, I can easily imagine rooms becoming overcrowded with big images. Given that you will be applying the Velcro Technique, each association will be on its own, and there will not be the problem of using too many objects, as long as each object is associated with their own trigger.

Not only rooms...

The example that we made was using a room in your house, but the great news is that any place you know will work. (Your office, your gym, your parents' house, your favourite restaurant, your favourite shop, and so on.)

Besides a room, another 'space' that will work perfectly is any journey that you know very well. For example, I know that—in order to get to the train station—I exit my building; cross the road; see a bridge on the left, but keep going; I then come to an empty shop, a burger place, a pizza place, a Lebanese restaurant and a pub; and then I get to the station. Those can all become triggers. If I need more, I will lengthen my journey: I will go inside the station and recall the places and reference points there; then I will move to the adjacent tube station, where I will go through the barriers and down the escalator to the platform; then I will get on the tube; and so on.

When you use a journey to get somewhere, what you can do is start from your home and associate your main topic with the end of the journey, so that you can easily recall which direction you had to take and how long your journey was.

PRO HACK The multi-layer room

One of the interesting applications that the Velcro–Palace technique allows is for you to memorise multi-layer pieces of information. Let's say you have an appointment with a potential client, and you decide to memorise as many details as possible about the conversation. You select your kitchen and you associate your client with the door. At that point he tells you that he has two children. You may associate the image of two children to the fridge-freezer. Then, he decides to share their names, so you associate an image for Mary with the fridge part, and an image for Tom with the freezer. But your potential client is really proud of his children, so he tells you that Mary loves reading and ballet, while Tom adores playing football. What can you do? You can associate the image of a book to the drinks in the door of the fridge; the image of the ballet to the vegetables in the fridge; and the image of a football with the ice creams in the freezer. And so on if necessary.

Of course, not every object can be split so many times. But, that said, you will be able to split them more than you think. (Even a bottle can be split into 'cap, label, bottle and liquid'.) When you cannot go further, just go on with your Velcro by using the last image as the trigger for the next one. The more you will have split, the easier your job will be.

You can already imagine how helpful this will turn out to be when you need to memorise Mind Maps (Chapter Thirteen).

Using the same place y/n

One of the big questions people raise about using the Memory Palace is whether it is fine to utilise the same place over and over again. 'Will I not get confused?' they ask.

The reality is that, if you do not apply the Velcro Technique to the Memory Palace, then the risk of becoming confused is high—especially if you use the same place at very close intervals.

Only once you commit your information to the long-term memory (Chapter Nineteen) are you free to use the place again.

However, when you use the Velcro–Palace Technique, things are different.

Overall, I would recommend you use different places when memorising the same topic. Yet I concede that there are times in which this is not possible. In such cases, applying one of the following measures will prevent you from getting confused.

The first one is by using different background colours for different topics. If I have to use my kitchen again, I could 'paint' my triggers in red the second time round in order to distinguish it. This strategy works well if you are good with colours. I am not, though I am sharing it with you because I have some clients who have found it extremely helpful. For me, the risk of getting confused would still be very high, so I prefer to use the second strategy.

In this case what you do is employ different main characters, who go around the room interacting with the same objects, creating a common thread that will leave no room for doubt.

Words: 1,179 (from Heads Up)   *Time (in seconds):* _____

A short example will clarify what I mean.

Let's say you want to memorise something related to the Romans, something related to astronomy and something related to anatomy: all in your bathroom. First of all, find an image for all these topics, and make sure it is an image that can take actions (do not select a place, for example; instead, people, animals and objects—especially if anthropomorphic—will work). You could find a gladiator for the Romans, a talking moon for astronomy and a skeleton for anatomy.

OBJECT	SPEECH ON ROME	PLANETS	HEART
SINK	Colosseum	Mercury	Fist
BATHTUB	Julius Caesar	Venus	Chambers
TOILET	The die is cast	Earth	Layers

And so on.

For each object in your bathroom, you will have three different associations. So, to make sure that you do not get confused, you will use the image you selected for the topic as your *main character*, taking very different actions. For example:

> *The gladiator looks at the sink and notices the Colosseum is in it, so he jumps in. The gladiator sees that Julius Caesar is having a bath and so he brings him a Caesar salad, but Caesar chokes. The gladiator throws a die into the toilet and he scores a six, but then he flushes it and loses the die.*
>
> *An astronaut opens the sink and mercury comes out and covers everything. The astronaut takes a bath and paints The Birth of Venus on the wall. The astronaut wants to push the Earth down the toilet, but the Earth is too big, and so it is safe. It then pushes him away.*
>
> *An anthropomorphic heart tries to punch the water of the sink with his fist, but he misses and hits the basin instead. The same heart enters the bathtub and gets divided into four chambers. The heart finds a huge three-layer cake on the toilet but when he gets closer to eat it he falls into the toilet.*

These are examples to let you understand how to use it, and even though you will probably not have to memorise these words, you can see that it will be impossible to get confused between a gladiator jumping into the Colosseum and the element mercury coming out of the sink; just as I would be most surprised if you were to mix up a gladiator rolling a die into the toilet and a heart trying to eat a cake.

To practise, I will now give you two lists of ten words to associate to the same objects:

LIST 1	LIST 2
Fish tank	TV
Kite	Hairdryer
Hospital	Bench
Stone	Nun
Helmet	Gold
Daisy	Snake
Sofa	Skate
Orange	Umbrella
Cat	Stake
Vacuum cleaner	Dress

How did it go?

The Velcro–Palace technique will help you become so fast that you will not recognise yourself (in a good sense). Build your palaces by selecting the objects you want to use in the different places you know, and you will be set to go.

CHAPTER SEVENTEEN

Numbers (and Codes)

[Desk is better]

The reason why we need a separate section to talk about numbers and codes is that numbers and codes are those pieces of abstract information that are the hardest to picture. During this section you are going to learn some techniques that will allow you to easily remember any number or code you please—without getting confused and while also having some fun!

As this is a part that requires more effort than others, you will need to lay a foundation before you can apply it. If you do not have the time right now, and you just need to remember numbers from one to ten, you can skip to Chapter Seventeen and its passage on 'Up to Ten'). However, if you know that you may someday need to remember higher numbers, keep on reading: taking time to build the foundation will be worth the effort. To clarify: when I speak of numbers I am referring to things like your credit card number; your partner's date of birth; figures and percentages in your field of work; formulae; PIN codes and passwords; and so on.

The concept is very simple: as usual, what you need to do is to turn any piece of information you need to remember into a tangible image. And the same will work for numbers, so that you can apply the Velcro Technique. There are some numbers for which this process may be easy to remember (your date of birth, the number of the jersey of your favourite player, 007). But what you need is to find a system that will allow you to remember *all* numbers, not just some here and there. We are about to build it, so get ready for the journey.

This is a Road to Mastery layer, and will require some effort from your part. If you do not need many numbers and you would rather work on a No Effort layer, you can jump to Verbal Hooks (Chapter Seventeen).

Words: 328   Time (in seconds): _____

The Phonetic System
{Road to Mastery layer}

The phonetic mnemonic system (also known as the Major System) has a lot of history. Dating back to the sixteenth century, it comes from the question that many intellectuals asked themselves as to how to remember numbers more efficiently. A lot of scientists and scholars attempted to create an effective system, and through the evolution of all their research the Major System was born. We can also call it the Hook System, as it is composed of hooks.

The basic concept of the Hook System is this: to turn a number into an image—and to be able to do this for *any* number—you need to create some words. This system allows you to have the flexibility of creating your own words, while at the same time respecting some rules that will prevent you from getting confused. We will build it one brick at a time, and you will become a master at memorising any sort of number. So fasten your seatbelt!

Brick One: the sounds

It all starts with the phonetic sounds. These are sounds that are associated with each figure, which you need to memorise.

Phonetic Sounds

1   **T, D, TH**
E.g.: tie, day, the...

2   **N**
E.g.: Noah, Ann, new

3   **M**
E.g.: Ma, ham, Amy

4   **R**
E.g.: ray, hour, arrow

5   **L**
E.g.: law, hole, all...

6   **CH, J, SH**
E.g.: each, jaw, shoe...

7   **K, G**
E.g.: cow, key, egg...

8   **F, V**
E.g.: fee, vow, view...

9   **P, B**
E.g.: pie, bee, boy...

0   **S, Z**
E.g.: ice, sea, zoo...

When you memorise them, make sure you memorise the sound, not the letter: because when it comes to phonetic sounds what matters is not how you write them but how they sound.

Now practise recalling them in both directions: starting from the sound to come up with the number and vice versa. As soon as you feel confident enough, move on to step two.

Brick Two: the rules

Whenever you use the phonetic sounds, you need to keep a few rules in mind to ensure their power is fully exploited.

As I mentioned in the previous section, with phonetic sounds what matters is not how you write them, but how they sound. This means that we will consider as 'sounds' only those sounds that we can hear and which we need to execute a complete or partial closure of the vocal tract to produce. All of this to say that every letter that produces a vowel sound (an open sound) will not be considered a sound (and is not in the list you have learned), so you will just skip it.

For each of the examples I will write, please try to write down the correct sounds before checking the answer, so that you can practise and automate the use of phonetic sounds.

1. SULTAN—_ _ _ _
2. BOOK—_ _
3. ROCKET—_ _ _
4. CHEF—_ _

Special letters

There are some letters that may be a bit tricky, so write your best guess then check the answers at the end of the section and we can analyse them together.

5. GHOST—_ _ _
6. ENOUGH—_ _
7. THOUGH—_

Here we find GH in all three words, yet it is pronounced in different ways. Remember that what matters is how the word sounds: never get tricked by the spelling!

8. CERTAIN—_ _ _ _
9. CURTAIN—_ _ _ _

What happens here? We have two words that are spelled with the same consonants, but pronounced differently. Always mind the pronunciation!

10. HAWAII
11. YOU

No, it was not a mistake not to give you the space for the sounds. These words have no phonetic sound!

12. GOING—_ _
13. MOTHER—_ _ _

In this case, you may have disagreed with the sounds that we have selected. Do not worry, at times it happens. The reality is that -ng and -r are two sounds that are pronounced very differently according to what English accent you have. As a general rule in the book, we will follow that -ng is 2 and -r is always 4. But you are free to personalise this rule according to your pronunciation!

14. TAXI—_ _ _

The letter 'x' is pronounced as the combination of 'k' and 's' (if you struggle to hear it, pronounce the word taxi as slowly as you can). As a result, it is the only letter that will include more than one sound.

Doubles

15. TELL—_ _

Here, as you can see, we have a double letter. If you pronounce 'tell' with one, two or fifteen Ls, your tongue will still hit your palate only the once. So, every time you encounter a double, it will count as one.

Solutions

1. 0512; 2. 97; 3. 471; 4. 68; 5. 701; 6. 28; 7. 1; 8. 0412; 9. 7412; 10. none; 11. none; 12. 72; 13. 314; 14. 170; 15. 15.

Brick Three: some practice

Now that you have learned all the rules, it is time to put them into practice. On top of each word in the following extract, write down the correct numbers to help you become more fluent with the phonetic sounds.

Extract from *Jonathan Livingston Seagull* by Richard Bach

IT WAS MORNING, AND THE NEW SUN SPARKLED GOLD across the ripples of a gentle sea.

A mile from shore a fishing boat chummed the water, and the word for Breakfast Flock flashed through the air, till a crowd of a thousand seagulls came to dodge and fight for bits of food. It was another busy day beginning.

But way off alone, out by himself beyond boat and shore, Jonathan Livingston Seagull was practising. A hundred feet in the sky he lowered his webbed feet, lifted his beak, and strained to hold a painful hard twisting curve through his wings. The curve meant that he would fly slowly, and now he slowed until the wind was a whisper in his face, until the ocean stood still beneath him. He narrowed his eyes in fierce concentration, held his breath, forced one... single... more... inch... of... curve... Then his feathers ruffled, he stalled and fell.

Seagulls, as you know, never falter, never stall. To stall in the air is for them disgrace and it is dishonour.

But Jonathan Livingston Seagull, unashamed, stretching his wings again in that trembling hard curve—slowing, slowing, and stalling once more—was no ordinary bird.

Most gulls do not bother to learn more than the simplest facts of flight—how to get from shore to food and back again. For most gulls, it is not flying that matters, but eating. For this gull, though, it was not eating that mattered, but flight. More than anything else, Jonathan Livingston Seagull loved to fly.

This kind of thinking, he found, is not the way to make one's self popular with other birds. Even his parents were dismayed as Jonathan spent whole days alone, making hundreds of low-level glides, experimenting.

He didn't know why, for instance, but when he flew at altitudes less than half his wingspan above the water, he could stay in the air longer, with less effort. His glides ended not with the usual feet-down splash into the sea, but with a long flat wake as he touched the surface with his feet tightly streamlined against his body. When he began sliding into feet-up landings on the beach, then pacing the length of his slide in the sand, his parents were very much dismayed indeed.

'Why, Jon, *why?* his mother asked. 'Why is it so hard to be like the rest of the flock, Jon? Why cannot you leave low flying to the pelicans, the albatross? Why do not you *eat?* Jon, you're bone and feathers!'

'I do not mind being bone and feathers, Mum. I just want to know what I can do in the air and what I cannot, that's all. I just want to know.'

Brick Four: the words

Turning words into numbers will not find many applications (even though you can have fun sending some coded messages every now and then). However, in the same way in which you can translate words into numbers, you can do the opposite, which—quite frankly—will be much more helpful to help you memorise things. If I say to you 4, what words come to mind whose sounds would convert to only number 4? 4 is *r*, so it could be ray, hair, row, air, hour, our, arrow, where, and so on. What if I tell you 17? 1 is *t, d, th* and 7 is *k, g*—so you will need to consider possible combinations between the sounds for 1 and the sounds for 7. For example, you could come up with taco, tuck, duck, dig, dug, thick, dog, and so on.

This requires a little practise, especially if you are not used to playing with puzzles and codes. I am going to write a few numbers here for you to practise on: write at least one word per group of numbers.

72 _____   321 _____
31 _____   952 _____
58 _____   714 _____
94 _____   351 _____
60 _____   841 _____

Brick Five: the hooks

You are now able to create words from numbers, which is exactly what we said we needed in order to memorise numbers easily. We will now take this slightly further by merging this concept with the principle of triggers. Very often, the numbers that you will memorise will be triggers for new bits of information. Triggers are our pillars: they must be easy to come up with it, fast, and, most importantly, stable. If every time you have a number you use different images to represent it, you will waste precious time and miss out on the advantage that triggers provide by virtue of their being stable and unchangeable.

Do not despair, there is a solution for this—the Hook System.

The Hook System is a collection of images for all the numbers from one to ninety-nine (created using their phonetic sounds), which you will always use to picture the number they represent.

In the previous exercise you will have noticed that, for almost every number combination, more than one word could work. The purpose of having your Hook System is to choose one word that fits two characteristics, and to use that word *all the time*, so that for your mind it will become automatic to associate that number to that word.

The two characteristics are as follows: the word needs to respect the correct phonetic sounds, and it needs to be an image you can picture. As long as you follow these two rules, you can be as creative as you like.

For example, 1 could be converted into tea, tie, dough, the, die, dye, and so on. Some of these are abstract, so you can discard them directly, while others could all work. Which one is the best? It does not matter. As long as it is tangible, it will work. In this case we will use tea.

Using the same principle, number 2 will be Noah, number 3 ma and so on. I will attach a list of all the hooks from 1 to 99, but what I suggest to my clients is that they create their own hooks, so they become easier to recall and picture. The only ones that you should learn from this list are the ones from one to ten, and the reason will become clear when we see the different options we have for memorising lists. For all the others, you can either use that suggested here or create a new one.

The Hook System

1 Tea
2 Noah
3 Ma'
4 Ray
5 Law
6 Shoe
7 Cow
8 Vow
9 Bee
10 Toes
11 Teddy
12 Tuna
13 Time
14 Tyre
15 Tail
16 Tissue
17 Taco
18 TV
19 Tape
20 Nose

21 Net
22 Nun
23 Nemo
24 Narrow
25 Nail
26 Inch
27 Neck
28 Knife
29 Knob
30 Mouse
31 Mat
32 Moon
33 Mummy
34 Hammer
35 Mail
36 Match
37 Mic
38 Movie
39 Map
40 Rose

41 Road
42 Rain
43 Rum
44 Roar
45 Rail
46 Rich
47 Rock
48 Roof
49 Rope
50 Lace
51 Lid
52 Lane
53 Lime
54 Lorry
55 Lily
56 Lash
57 Lake
58 Love
59 Lip
60 Cheese

61 Chat
62 Chain
63 Gym
64 Cherry
65 Jail
66 Cha Cha
67 Cheek
68 Chef
69 Chip
70 Case
71 Cat
72 Gun
73 Gum
74 Car
75 Koala
76 Cash
77 Cake
78 Coffee
79 Cab
80 Face

81 Photo
82 Fan
83 Foam
84 Fire
85 Fall
86 Fish
87 Fog
88 Fifa
89 Vape
90 Pizza
91 Boat
92 Bone
93 Puma
94 Beer
95 Ball
96 Bush
97 Bike
98 Beef
99 Baby
100 Daisies

If, among the numbers from one to ninety-nine, there are any you are already associated with, do not bother creating a hook using the phonetic sounds: you already have your hook! For example, I know several people that, for number 23, use either Michael Jordan or LeBron James. This is perfectly fine, as you are so associated with that number that you are sure to not get confused with any other.

You can easily understand how using a Hook System will make your life easier. There will be no more getting confused between 67 and 76, because the image of a cheek is completely different from the image of a cage.

Any time in which you need to remember a code, a credit card number, an address, or even just a percentage that could impress someone during a presentation, all you will need to do is to use the correct hook/s and apply the Velcro Technique.

Brick Six: Velcro Technique and having fun

Once your hooks have been learned, you can start using them applying the Velcro Technique. The images of your hooks will work exactly as any other image you would use to memorise anything else.

Let's say you want to memorise your debit card PIN code 7694. What you will do is to follow the Velcro Technique.

1. Trigger. Find an image for your debit card. It could be the image of the card itself or the logo of the bank that issued it (make sure you picture it vividly so that you will not get confused with other cards or banks).

2. New Information. Find your hooks for 76 and 94 (for example cage and beer).

3. PAV. Create a PAV association between your image for debit card and your image for 76, and then continue by associating 76 with 94.

4. Lock. Make sure there is a final action to fix the image of 94.

5. Visualise. Picture the whole association in your mind.

Given that you will probably need your pin code in the future, what you can then do is to apply the long-term memorisation technique (Chapter Nineteen), so you can access the information at any time.

Let's have some fun

Once you have all the bricks, you can have fun applying this technique to anything you need, or even just for practice. Here are some ideas.

One exercise that will help you practise the Velcro Technique and the Hooks is memorising a very long number. You can take Pi for example, and start from its first twenty decimal places, or you could memorise your credit card number.

You can memorise a series of dates associated with events.

You could take a list of kings or presidents and memorise the dates in which they reigned or were in office.

Your only limit is your imagination.

PRO HACK Does knowing your hooks really make a difference?

At times people believe that memorising all the hooks up to one hundred will take too much time, relative to how often they will need to use them. Memorising all the one hundred hooks should not take long, but it may be true that—if you never run into numbers—you may not want to invest that time.

What you can do instead is to become very good at improvising hooks by inventing them on the spot, so that if you ever want to remember a PIN code or the price of one item you know how and can do so quickly.

How to remember lists of ten items: the Multiplier

{Easy Peasy layer} and {Road to Mastery layer}

Over the years, I also found myself working with people who had very few numbers to remember in life, but who had a series of lists of items to remember in order. At times the Velcro–Palace will do; other times, for some small lists, you may want to use the hooks everyone has their own preferences, and in most cases you are free to choose.

However, when you need to learn a lot of different lists, you want to make sure that you do not get confused. So here is a collection of different strategies you can use to memorise lists of ten items. Try them all, and have fun with them! The first two will use the phonetic sounds, while the following ones can be used also if you are yet to have learned the phonetic sounds.

Alternative hooks with 'H'

{Road to Mastery layer}

You may recall that Hs do not count as a phonetic sound, so the first strategy will be to create hooks that are different from the ones you have learnt with the Hook System, and that will start with a H. Given these all start with a H, it will be easy for you to recall the right set of hooks without getting confused.

Alternative hooks with zero

{Road to Mastery layer}

Another strategy you can use is to mentally add a 'zero' before the digits, and create hooks for 01, 02, 03 and so on.

Verbal hooks

{Easy Peasy layer}

Another set of hooks from one to ten can be created focusing on the sound of the number rather than the phonetic sounds.

Yes, phonetic sounds are the fastest and safest way to remember any number, as they allow you quick access to an image for any number without creating confusion between similar numbers. However, if you only need to memorise numbers up to ten and you do not want to bother memorising the phonetic sounds (or you want to save learning them for later), you can use this strategy.

Graphic hooks
{Easy Peasy layer}

Another set of hooks up to ten, which you also can create if you want to leave the memorisation of the phonetic sounds for later, is to find hooks that look like the different digits.

NUMBERS (AND CODES)

1.	Hat		1.	Suit
2.	Hen		2.	Sign
3.	Ham		3.	Sumo
4.	Hair		4.	Sahara
5.	Hell		5.	Soul
6.	Hitch		6.	Sushi
7.	Hook		7.	Sock
8.	Hive		8.	Sofa
9.	Hippo		9.	Soap
0.	Hose		0.	S.O.S

1.	Bun		1.	
2.	Shoe		2.	
3.	Tree		3.	
4.	Door		4.	
5.	Dive		5.	
6.	Sticks		6.	
7.	Heaven		7.	
8.	Gate		8.	
9.	Vine		9.	
0.	Hen		10.	

One to five
{Easy Peasy layer}

If your list is up to five items, you can also use your hand as a hook.

- 1 = Thumb—thumb up
- 2 = Index finger—pointed at someone
- 3 = Middle finger—no explanation needed!
- 4 = Ring finger—a ring
- 5 = Pinkie finger—promise

Alphanumeric Codes and Symbols
{Easy Peasy layer}

There are times in which you will need to remember an alphanumeric code. In that case the process will be the same, but you will need to find images starting from the letters.

Another application that a lot of people struggle with (unless they use memory techniques) is remembering formulae. The reason for this is simple: memorising a formula means remembering a mixture of numbers, letters and symbols: it is the ultimate abstract information. It is one thing to memorise a short formula, but once you have more than one to remember—and those are similar and/or complex—confusion awaits.

However, if it is true that a formula has tougher elements to it in terms of memorisation, the real difference between a phone number and a formula is that a phone number is a series of *random* digits, while a formula is the representation of a concept that you can *understand*. This actually makes remembering formulae easier than remembering phone numbers. So, always remember to start by understanding the formula and only then memorising it: it will be so much simpler that way.

And if you struggle to understand it in the first place, go and check out how to improve your understanding (Chapter Eleven).

NUMBERS (AND CODES)

Here are a collection of images you can use to convert letters and symbols into something you can picture. From the examples you may notice that there are different strategies you can apply: based on the sound, the shape or the meaning of the letter or symbol. Discover which one works best for you: taking inspiration from these examples but feeling free to adapt them to your preference.

GENIUS BY CHOICE

Letters

	Upper Case			Lower Case			Greek	
	A	B	C	a	b	c	A α	
Shape	△△△	(figure)	⚓	🐌	👢	🎧	B β	🦋
Name	Andrew	Barbara	Charles	-	-	-	Γ γ	
Object (Big for Upper, Small for Lower)	✈	⛵	🚗	🦋	🎈	💳	Δ δ	

Numbers
Use the hook system

10^2 E.g. A tiny **Noah** jumping on some massive **toes**

$\overset{20}{\underset{6}{\uparrow}}$ Roof

E.g. On top of the roof there is a massive **nose**, under there is a red **shoe**

Symbols
*Use the **shape** or the image of the **idea** they represent*

+   ✚ Adding something
-    🗡 Removing something
×   🌀 (windmill)
/   🗼
=   🚃
√   〰

( )   ◖ Room
[ ]   📺 Building
{ }   🎻 City

CHAPTER EIGHTEEN

Applications (Trigger–New Information)

[Desk is better]

Now that you have learned the ABC of memory, it will be a matter of putting together the elements you need in order to memorise whatever information you run into. Whether it is a mind map, a formula, a phone number, a presentation, a name or anything else, the process will be the same. Remember to access your gift at geniusbychoice.co.uk/gift, so you can start understanding how to deepen the techniques for important applications such as learning languages and specific exams.

For each of the applications that follow, all you need to do is to follow this process.

1. Find your trigger
2. Analyse the new information: is it better to use a simple Velcro or a Velcro Palace? Do you have any numbers involved? (If so, use the Hook System)
3. PAV
4. Lock the PAV
5. Visualise

Enjoy!

Type of Info	Trigger	New Info
Foreign Word	Image of the meaning	Foreign word
Historical Date	Event	Date
Name	Face	Name
Formula	Title of the formula	Formula (numbers, letters and symbols)
Phone Number	Image of Owner	Phone number
Document	Image of document	Title of the formula
Credit Card	Bank or card	Number/Expiry date etc
Birthday	Birthday person with a present	Date
Phone Pin Code	Phone with a pin	Code
Credit Card Pin Code	Card with a pin	Code
Capital	Country	Capital
Quotation	Meaning of the quote	Exact words and author
Element	Atomic number	Element and its details
Dance Move and Yoga Pose	Name of the move/pose	Each object of the room a pose
Direction	Destination	Each object of the room a direction
Presentation	Topic	Each object of the room a sentence
Definition	Word	Definition word by word
Meeting	Person/topic of the meeting	Date

CHAPTER NINETEEN

Long-Term Memorisation

[Bed is fine]

So far you have learned how to memorise huge amounts of data quickly and precisely, with an added dose of fun. But quick and precise are not enough if you then forget what you have learned.

I always found it so frustrating when I would study something and get a good result, only to end up not remembering most of the details a few days later. I could not make sense of it: how was it possible for all that information to just slip away? Was it a matter of limited capacity in our brains? Or was it my fault?

The only reason you do not remember everything you want to is because you have not trained your mind to do so. Have you watched the Pixar movie *Inside Out*? It contains a very interesting scene in which the storage area where all memories are kept gets swept out overnight; those that are no longer needed being cleaned away.

Somehow, our brain works in a similar way. It selects what we want to keep and removes what we 'do not need'. How does this selection process happen, though? If the connection is very strong, your mind will keep the information; if the connection is weak, your mind will let it go.

Markedly emotional events stay in our memory without us needing to do anything because the connection that is created when they occur is extremely strong.

When you memorise something through repetition, the connection will be very weak; so weak, in fact, that after few hours it will start to come undone.

Applying the Genius PRIME Method, you will notice that your memory will already last longer, because the active process you have put in place to memorise concepts and details creates a stronger initial connection. However, if you do not actively apply a technique to commit memory to the long term, sooner or later you will end up forgetting some or most of what you have memorised.

Do not despair—there is a simple but effective way to prevent this. It will require an investment of five to ten minutes per every hour of study. It is up to you to choose whether to invest those minutes or not, according to whether you do or do not wish to remember that information in the future.

And if you are wondering whether your brain will be able to store all the things that you would like to retain forever, then fear not: a 2010 article in *Scientific American* estimated the brain's capacity to be around 2.5 petabytes (2.5 million gigabytes), so you are very unlikely to fill it up.

Words: 439　　　　　　　　　　*Time (in seconds):* _____

The evolution of Spaced Repetition: Timed Recalls
{Easy Peasy layer}

Spaced Repetition—Y or N

Spaced repetition is a technique that has been proven to be very effective in enhancing your long-term retention. The concept is simple. A few minutes after you finish your study session, your memory is at its best—one hundred per cent—and it will stay there for three to four hours. As time goes by it will plunge, until in a couple of days it will be at around (on average) thirty per cent.

If when you are about to forget something, you re-see it, then your mind will think that it is important and will remember it for longer. Therefore, by spacing your repetition of the information, you will be able to commit it to the long-term memory.

Traditional spaced repetition is very effective, but the way it is usually explained misses one very important detail that will make a huge difference, especially if you apply the Velcro Technique and the Hourglass Technique. Welcome to the Timed Recalls.

Why Recalls?

A recall is very different from a revision.

You usually revise things before a test/performance, and the reason why you revise is because you are not sure you know the information. If you have a doubt about this, think about the following question: if tomorrow you had a test on your date of birth, the colour of your eyes and your name, would you need to revise all day long? Probably not. But, unfortunately, it is rare for us to have that level of certainty about our knowledge. How do you revise? Most people go over their notes again, re-reading through them a bit faster than before, but with what is called a passive method—as your eyes could easily be reading through your notes while your mind is thinking about something else. This is why 'repetition' is not enough. You need to use a recall.

Recalls are different from repetition and revision because they are *active*. In order to recall something, you need to look at the Trigger and come up with the New Information, or vice versa. When you are recalling concepts from your labels and keywords, your Trigger will be the label/keyword, while your New Information will be the concept that that label/keyword represents.

This process of actively coming up with the information you need will allow you to strengthen your connections, and every time you recall that piece of information your memory will last longer.

Why Timed?

In order to recall something actively, you need to do it when your memory is still at one hundred per cent. Therefore, there are some specific moments in which you will stage your recalls.

The first one will be in the window that comes between thirty minutes and three-to-four hours after you have finished studying. For convenience, we will say after one hour.

By recalling it after one hour, you allow your memory to last for one day. And so then, after one day or less, you will recall it again.

By doing so, the memory will be extended to last for a week. And so then, after one week or less, you will recall it again.

At that point, you will be fine for one month. And so then, after one month or less, you will recall it one more time.

If you never use that information again, you will need to recall it again after six months, and then after that once every year; but if you do use it then you will not need to recall it anymore.

Besides the fact you schedule the recalls for specific set times in the future, there is one more reason why they are called 'timed', which is that recalls are meant to be very fast. Remember that you will be first recalling your information at a time in which you still know ninety-five to a hundred per cent of the information, and so it will not be like when you attempt to revise something and find yourself struggling to come up with what you are supposed to remember. Instead, it will simply consist of thinking about that information that you already know. For a sense of the time required, recalling ninety words will take between seven and ten minutes.

The most important

The most important recall is the one you do after one hour. The reason for this is very simple but very important. After one hour you are supposed to remember the information one hundred per cent. This means that it represents your reality check: if after one hour you remember the detail or concept, it means that by simply following the planned Timed Recalls going forward you will be able to remember it forever; yet if after one hour you are hesitant and you struggle to come up with your detail or concept, it means that you need to adjust something in terms of how you learned it.

If what you cannot recall is a detail that you have memorised with the Velcro Technique, it means that you have skipped one of the five steps. If it is a concept that you squeezed into a label/keyword with the Hourglass Technique, it means that you need to re-read that paragraph and understand the concept better, so you can select a more effective label/keyword.

In both cases, there is absolutely nothing to despair about: it is better to catch a gap one hour on, rather than on the day of your performance itself! And the more you apply the Genius PRIME Method, the more you will notice that your recall precision will improve.

How precise with the timing?

When I say one hour, one day, one week and one month, I do so because it is simpler to remember. You can be flexible with the timings, thought you should never exceed the exact time by too much. If you cannot do it on the exact milestone, it is better to do it a bit before rather than a bit after.

As far as the first one goes, it may be that you cannot do it exactly one hour after. And that is not a problem. We know that your memory—even without memory techniques—stays at one hundred per cent for three to four hours, and with memory techniques even longer. This means that you can recall what you have learned up to five or six hours later. If you do not want to waste time, do not go beyond this, else—in case there is a detail that you do not remember—it will be impossible for you to know whether there was something wrong in your application of the Velcro Technique or simply too much time had passed by since you learned it.

The main mistakes

There are two mistakes you can make in relation to your recalls.

The first one is that, when the time for your recall comes, you may think 'I feel I still know the information, I do not need to recall it'. Well, this is understandable because you have always been used to revising things when you were uncertain about remembering them. Yet in this case, remember that you are supposed to still remember it: otherwise, how could you do an *active* recall? So, if you feel you still know it, even better: you will be faster at recalling it.

The other mistake you may fall into is this. Imagine you look at your Trigger with the intention of coming up with the New Information, but you struggle to recall what you have memorised. So you check what the New Information is, and you suddenly remember the PAV association you had made. You think 'Right, now I remember!', and you move on. Can you think of why this is a mistake? Because there is a difference between recognition and recall. When you see a piece of information that you have stored in your memory, you may be able to recognise what it is (think about true/false or multiple choice questions); but, if you do not train your recall abilities, then when you need to actively come up with the right detail—and are not faced with the options to choose from—you will be unable to do so. When we live, we are not usually faced with several options from which we need to choose, but instead need to come up with the information actively. This is why, if your recognition is ok but your recall is not there, you need to improve your Velcro or understand the concept better.

NOTE:
Every time you recall the information, your memory will evolve, and there will be a moment in which you will be able to recall what you have learned with the Velcro Technique without thinking about your PAV association anymore. This happens because the Velcro Technique allows you to create the scaffolding you need in order to put up your building, but once the building is up, the scaffolding can be dropped and you are left with the building (memory) with no scaffolding (PAV) anymore. This is important to keep in mind: the stronger your PAV association is, the sooner you will drop the scaffolding. I have learned most of my English vocabulary using the Velcro Technique, and if I had to think about each PAV association every time I speak, people would find me crazy!

Words: 1,574   *Time (in seconds):* _____

Inspiration Time from Our Genius Alumni

I am a current MSc Nutrition student in UCL. When I was studying for my bachelor degree I spent a lot of time studying and preparing for my exams but I wasn't able to retain the information a few days after the exam. I decided to take the course to prepare for my master course wanting to put the learnt information into long-term memory.

I found the Genius in 21 Days course super useful. I now manage to spend less time studying but I am able to remember information a long time afterwards. My exam results during my MSc Nutrition gradually improved and I got a distinction in my latest module!

Studying has been more fun since applying the techniques as it allows me to bring my creative side out and I enjoy it so much that I spend more time studying than I did whilst I was studying for my bachelor degree.

I loved reading when I was younger but when I got older I didn't read as much as I found reading took a lot of my time. After the course, my reading speed increased a lot after using the techniques they taught. I went from spending a month to read a book during my spare time to now spending less than a week to read a book leisurely. It really helped me to find my passion for reading again and I have read many more books since then.

I have grown so much during these past months, I am now more confident and more determined to go out and pursue my dreams.

I would like to thank all the Mentors in Genius in 21 Days who have been the most supportive throughout the entire time. Their passion and their stories have touched and impacted me and many others to not only want to improve ourselves but to do more and help other people achieve greatness as well.

Alfred Chan - University Student

PART V.
EXPRESS

Expression is the final phase of your learning process. Very rarely do we study things for the sole purpose of knowing them; most of the time we will want to use the information we have learned.

There are a lot of different ways in which you may need to express your knowledge.

Some of them will require no effort other than simply applying what you have learned. For instance speaking a language; using whichever new knowledge you have acquired to increase your competence; remembering some details you have memorised in order to be more efficient at work; recalling the name of your client's kids. You get the gist.

However, there are other contexts in which expressing your new knowledge may not be as straightforward.

When you are preparing for an exam, your expression will be the exam itself. When you are preparing for a talk, you will have to present in front of people. When you need to attend a job interview, it is there you will need to prove your knowledge.

In all these cases, knowing things very well will not be enough—you need to *prove* that you know them.

Performing under stress comes very easily to some people, but for the majority it does not. When you are nervous, what happens to your body? Your heart starts beating faster, your hands get sweaty, your mouth dries up. Is it always easy to perform at your best in this state? Not at all. Your lucidity vanishes, your thoughts become less clear. There may be things that you knew ten minutes before (and that you suddenly remember ten minutes after), but in the moment of the performance they just slip your mind.

Unfortunately, in all these situations the person evaluating you is not able to assess how hard you have worked to prepare, nor how well you actually know your stuff, because all they can evaluate is how well you perform.

This is why it is of paramount importance to learn how to manage your stress, so that crucially you can perform at your best when you are under pressure—ensuring that what comes across is not how nervous you are but how prepared you are.

A little note for those of you who are learning new things but do not have to perform to prove their preparation. The tips I am going to share here could benefit your whole preparation, not just the final performance: so have a read, it will be very helpful!

Words: 416　　　　　　　　　　*Time (in seconds):* _____

CHAPTER TWENTY

Peak Performance

[Bed is fine]

Performing well under pressure—surprisingly for most—is not an innate ability. And contrary to what the majority of people think, it does not depend (solely) on how well you can lower your heart rate during your performance. It is a skill that is built, step after step: from the very first moment you learn what your performance will be.

For the sake of simplicity, I will be using the word 'performance' indiscriminately, regardless of what kind of performance you need to deal with. It could be an exam, a presentation, a job interview, being questioned by your boss, performing on a stage, and so on. Any activity in which you need to showcase your preparation will from here onwards be called a 'performance'.

Words: 124   *Time (in seconds):* _____

News Time
{Easy Peasy layer}

This is the time in which you find out about what you will need to do, and is a crucial step towards how well you will perform. Some of you may be surprised by this, and will ask 'How can the moment in which I receive the news about my goal affect how stressed I will be during the performance?'

To explain it to you I need to share a concept: one that you may have already heard about, yet will have probably never related to performance.

Confirmation Bias and Internal Dialogue

Do you like being right? If you answered yes, you will be happy, because you are right. If you answered no, then I am sorry to break it to you, but you are lying. I am not a diviner, and I may not know you personally, but I know that all human beings love being right, regardless of them wanting to or not.

Once you have an opinion about something, if you do not do anything about it and leave it as it is, your mind will automatically start looking for proof that what you believe is right. Your mind will want to be so right that it will be ready to discard any piece of information which does not confirm the initial thought, leading you to overlook some details that may be of utter importance.

When this initial thought is productive and empowering, this mechanism is almost harmless (and at times it even plays in your favour, as we will see); however, when your initial thought is a doubtful or fearful one, this bias will undermine your whole preparation and your performance, increasing your nervousness and stress. In the best case, you will not enjoy your study process; in the worst, you will fail your performance.

Because of this, you need to be extremely careful about *what* you want to prove right. Not paying attention to this means leaving your performance to chance.

The reason why your first thought will affect your performance so strongly is because it will generate a certain kind of internal dialogue, which will either give you energy and focus or create tension and fear. Fear and confusion are the two main enemies of a great performance, and they feed on your negative internal dialogue.

Managing the Bias

If your confirmation bias is so strong, how can you prevent it from affecting your performance?

What you need to pay attention to is your first emotional reaction to the news about the performance. Is your body saying yes or no to it? Are you scared or excited? Are you aware of what it entails or over-optimistic? I say 'body' and not 'mind' because your mind can trick you, but your first visceral reaction cannot. Feeling that reaction and then analysing it in a detached way (here comes your scientific mind, again) will save you from the effect of the confirmation bias.

Your analysis may lead to a couple of different results.

If you are happy with your reaction, nourish these thoughts by also letting them sustain you during the most challenging moments.

If you are not happy with your thoughts, now is time to adjust them before they sabotage your result.

There are innumerable strategies and techniques to learn how to manage your thoughts so that they do not set you on a downward spiral. The ones that I am going to share here have won over others because they can be applied immediately: their 'value for time' is very high.

Change the questions

The internal dialogue that you have inside your mind works mostly with questions and answers. You ask a question; your mind finds an answer. When using Google, you input a word or sentence and it comes up with all the answers that match what you asked. When searching through information, your mind is like Google; slightly slower, maybe, but very similar. There is one detail, though, that has a huge impact on your results. Your mind can open multiple searches at the same time, a bit like if you opened Google in several different tabs or windows. Given that your mind is slower, however, its searches will last longer, and will continue to use your energy (and often part of your focus) even when you are doing something else, until a convincing answer is found. To make it simple to understand, think if something similar to what I am about to describe has ever happened to you. You are taking a shower, and all of a sudden you recall the name of the actor who was the main character in the movie you watched three days before. Maybe it was not an actor's name, but the title of that familiar melody you heard yesterday, or that word that had slipped your mind two days ago. You get the gist.

This happens because, in the time span between your question and your shower, your mind has continued searching for the answer, incessantly.

The problem is not really in the energy you use for it, but in the kind of question you ask yourself, for a very simple reason that I am going to illustrate now.

Imagine that you fail an exam or miss an important deadline you had, and you ask yourself 'Why do these bad things always happen to me?' Your mind will start its search to find an answer to this. And here we get to the most important part about questions. Behind almost every question lies an assumption that will make the real difference in the answer you will find. In a question like 'Why do these bad things always happen to me?', what is the assumption? There are many. The 'these things' of which you speak are labelled as 'bad', revoking every opportunity to turn them into good. They 'always' happen, as if only bad things can happen to you. They happen 'to' you, not 'for' you, so you are putting yourself in the role of a victim who is subject to external circumstances.

In the same situation you can ask yourself a different, more positive question, such as 'What can I learn from this situation?' There is an assumption here too: that something can be learnt. Maybe initially you do not understand what that something is, but remember: your mind will keep searching for the answer until it finds it. And one day you may be taking a shower when suddenly you find yourself having an aha moment, and thinking 'I know what I had to learn from that experience!'.

So how can you use the power of your questions? Whenever you catch yourself reacting negatively to the news, remember that that negative emotion comes from a question that you have asked yourself. Change the question, and the emotion will start to change.

The best kind of questions that you can introduce into your dialogue when you receive news surrounding an exam are questions that are not projected towards understanding why something happened or how hard it will be, but which are projected towards which resources you need to deal with it. If, at the news of a deadline/exam you feel scared, annoyed, incapable, frustrated, powerless (and so on), chances are you are focusing on how hard or time-consuming preparing for it will be. Your mind is not seeing either the advantage or the feasibility of the goal. If it is a matter of advantages, please see Chapter Three (passage on Motivation Sheet). If it is a matter of feasibility, it is time to change your questions. The list below will help point you towards the right kind of questions you should be asking:

- What resources do I need to excel at this?
- What talents can I use?
- How can I organise my activities to get it done?
- How can I have fun in the process?
- How will this allow me to become better?
- What skills will I be able to develop along the way?

Substitute

We said that questions carry with them important assumptions about life, about yourself, about others. One quick fix is to change the questions so that your mind can shift its focus. The other step you can take is to start breaking down those assumptions that are holding you back, and which are creating doubt, fear and confusion.

The reality is that most of those assumptions are nothing but that: assumptions. They are not the truth, they are not facts, and they are not meant to stay with you forever. Keeping them with you will only contribute to making your journey towards your goal more arduous. It will slow you down: making you feel more anxious and breaking down your confidence one step at a time. Given the confirmation bias, if you do not get rid of them you will soon start doubting yourself even more; feeling down; aiming lower, just to make sure you can achieve something; and probably not even managing to achieve those new mediocre goals, because mediocre goals never motivated anyone.

You must act and get rid of these assumptions. The reality, though, is that you cannot get rid of thoughts, nor hide them anywhere, as they are inside your brain and the more you think about them the stronger you make them. But what you can do is *substitute* them.

First of all, you need to remember that no event means anything other than what we decide it should mean. The same event experienced by different people means different things. Someone can receive a promotion and think they deserve it, while another person can receive a promotion and believe that no one else was around to get it instead of them. You may struggle to find a solution to a maths problem and think that math is really not your thing, while your friend may struggle to find a solution and believe they are missing an important detail in their knowledge. Nothing is true in itself (I am not talking about deep matters and truths in which you believe—this is not the place for that—but I am referring to all those assumptions we have about ourselves as learners).

Regardless of the nature of these assumptions (good or bad), they are a product of your imagination. Because of certain circumstances, when a certain event happened in your past, you decided to give it a certain meaning. At that point, your confirmation bias kicked in, and from that moment you started looking for (and finding) more and more references to that assumption, until it became your truth.

The good news is that, just in the same way you have created that assumption, you can uncreate it—or better, substitute it for a more effective one.

Taking inspiration from the concept of fixed vs growth mindset, which we discussed in Chapter Two, I will list here some of the most common assumptions people have, and what you can substitute them with.

Before changing them, however, you need to decide that you want to. Remember that our mind seeks comfort, and your old assumptions are extremely comfortable, as they give you (and probably have for years) the perfect excuse to be stressed about the future event, and therefore underperform. They are a shield that others can even find cute, so also attract a lot of sympathy for you from the people you care for. Are you willing to let this go in favour of a better emotional state and far better results?

Once you have decided you are up for the task, remember that your thoughts are just the crystallisation of a meaning you gave to a certain event. If you saw that event today—from the outside, with the awareness you have now—are you sure you would give it the same meaning? If you saw that little boy or girl that is restless because the maths teacher is boring, would you really tell him or her that 'Studying is not for you'? If you saw that teenager who blanked out during a presentation, would you really tell them 'You'll never speak in public again'? What if it was just a matter of finding your way to do it? What if it was just a matter of not knowing the best way for you to learn?

- I never seem to be able to keep my notes organised
  I have not found the best way to organise my notes

- I always fail when I have little time
  I want to learn how to achieve the goal in the time I have

- I work best when the deadline is almost there
  I can learn how to perform better when the pressure is not there

- I am so bad at this
  There are some skills I need to improve to become good at this

- It is going to be so boring
  How much fun I have depends on me

- That examiner is scary
  That examiner is a human being; the more competent I am, the less scary they will be

Words: 2,173   Time (in seconds): _____

Prep Time
{No Effort layer}

The prep time is likely to be the time that will last the longest. There is only a very quick thing to say about this. The more you do, the less time you have to overthink. If you have time to be scared and worried, it means you are not doing what you could in order to get ready. In that case, apply all the techniques we discussed in Chapter Three — Motivation to start acting now and get ready for your goal.

Words: 82   Time (in seconds): _____

Wait Time
{Easy Peasy layer}

The wait time is the moment between when you metaphorically close the book and when your performance comes. I know: at times you study up until the very last minute (or at least, you used to until now), so that you do not have much wait time between your preparation and performance. However, whether it is five minutes or one day, the wait time is the most troublesome phase for the majority of people. This is because nature does not like a vacuum; so if you do not fill it productively, this time will be filled by worry and fear. Read on to find out how to avoid this and, instead, use your wait as a boost for your performance.

Dream on

What people tend to do

We have already mentioned the importance of your internal dialogue, and you realise it often plays tricks on you: increasing your stress and magnifying your fears. Usually, when you are waiting for the performance, your mind tends to take you to places you would rather not go. 'What if I am asked one of the three things I have not properly understood?' What if the person assessing me is in a bad mood? What if I stutter? What if I blank out?'

In case you needed me to tell you, this is not a good way to use the time between your preparation and your performance.

What you can do instead

A better way to spend this time is by using the power of visualisation in your favour. When untamed, your mind can really take you to scary places; but, once utilised properly, it can become your greatest ally.

You may have already heard how important it is to visualise what you want. Athletes do it to enhance their performance, as do musicians, dancers and presenters.

But the question I get asked all the time is: How can you use visualisation well? You hear how you should visualise the best scenario, but is it really what will help you feel better? Will it not feel a bit fabricated?

I will give you my opinion on this, as I have probably tried most of the options suggested by books and coaches.

Visualisation is indeed fundamental, as it allows your mind to get to your performance ready. Imagine the first time in which you saw your boss. You may have been a bit nervous, and possibly not really at ease. Now, after the fiftieth time in which you see him or her, are you still that nervous? Probably not, because for your mind it is no longer something unknown, and is instead something you have learnt how to deal with.

Your performance works in the same way. The reason it may make you feel nervous right now (or at least one of the reasons) is that you have not done it enough times yet for your mind to feel comfortable with it. Visualisation can help in this.

A lot of studies have shown that, when you visualise something very vividly, it is almost impossible for your mind to distinguish it from real. You actually activate the same parts of the brain that you would activate if that thing were actually happening. The easiest example is to think about when you have a dream. You are sound asleep and you start having the worst nightmare; it feels so real that you wake up and you are shaken. Your body may even have accelerated your heartbeat, as if the peril were real. But it was just your imagination.

This is relevant to you because, if you use the power of visualisation, you will be able to visualise your performance in such detail that for your mind it will feel like it was happening. You may not be able to sit the same job interview fifty times, but surely you are able to visualise it fifty times. When you get to the 'real' job interview, for your mind it will no longer be the first time, but the fifty-first. A different kind of emotion.

How to do it well

I have heard many times that you should visualise only the best-case scenario, so that you can focus on the best vibe to attract the best situation to you. Although this may have some truth to it, for most people the best scenario seems so unlikely that their visualisation will be very superficial and useless.

Instead, what I suggest is this.

Close your eyes and breathe deeply to lower your brainwaves, and start picturing the performance from the moment in which you get to the place where it will happen. Your mind will take you somewhere. Make it as realistic as possible. If you know the room where it will happen or the faces you will see, make sure you include the details. If you do not, it does not matter, picture them as your mind wishes. If you visualise your performance as accurately as possible, there may be some unexpected situations that come up. Amazing. Picture how you want to react to them. Visualise how you want to react when the person in front of you seems unhappy with your performance; how you want to react when you have a moment of blank out; when you feel tense; or when you do not know the answer to something you are asked. Picture all the scenarios that come to mind.

As you deal with each situation, you will see that your confidence starts to rise, because you realise that you are getting ready for any circumstance. Remember that you cannot control other people's reactions, but you can definitely learn how to control yours.

This exercise will be a wonderful way to use your wait time, and as you do it you will realise that you are more and more ready. Enjoy!

Relax Productively

What people tend to do

During their wait time, some people tend to get increasingly stressed and nervous: going over notes, trying to perfect their competence, increasing their sense of a lack of preparation that will lead them to a poor performance.

What you can do instead

In that moment, keeping your mind on the performance will not do you much good. Instead, an alternative strategy that will help you immensely is to relax. And I do not mean sitting on the sofa while watching Netflix. I mean spending one day taking your mind off your performance completely. Go to a spa. Have a dinner party with friends. Go shopping. Do something that you love, which will distract you from your performance.

This injection of fun and relaxation will boost your results.

If you really cannot get your mind off it

If after having some fun your mind is still focused on the performance and cannot get some healthy relaxation, there is a better thing that you can do rather than frantically going through your notes or repeating things over and over again.

Recall what you know in an alternative way. Create a mind map (Chapter Thirteen) that includes everything you want to cover; read articles that are apparently unrelated but that contribute to increasing your background knowledge; ask a friend to discuss the topic if you know they have an opinion on it. Do something that is not exactly linked to revising passively but that gives you the impression you are getting more and more ready for your performance.

And then get some good sleep.

Words: 1,242   Time (in seconds): _____

Showtime

{Easy Peasy layer}

Finally, here we are. Showtime has come. If you have used your News Time, Prep Time and Wait Time to your advantage, your Showtime will be pure enjoyment—the moment in which you will share your knowledge, conveying your message in the best possible way.

However, even when you have prepared carefully, emotions may take over. There are two aspects that you will need to keep in mind, and, while you read on, you may see that you need the first, the second, or both. As usual, begin immediately applying what will make a difference for you, and then refine with the rest.

Energy first

Imagine a warrior who needs to prepare for a battle. Would you suggest that they sit scared and worried, or keep their energy so high that they are ready for anything? For their chances of survival, I would hope the latter. It is true that your performance is probably not a battle, but the same principle applies. If you spend the time before your performance worrying and frantically reviewing your notes, your emotional state will not be ready to perform at your best. Using your final minutes to instead increase your energy via some simple steps will make a huge difference to your result. Imagine how it would be to face the performance with the energy you get when you have just received a promotion, or when your favourite team has won a game, or when you have just received the wonderful news you were waiting for (pick the example that is more applicable to you).

I have selected two techniques to help you enter that emotional state. Both are simple to carry out and extremely effective.

Breathe

Over the years I have become familiar with a lot of breathing techniques. Breathing is closely related to many mental, physical and emotional reactions. If you think about it, you can tell a lot about how a person is feeling from their breathing. This is because your emotions affect the way you breathe. What is amazing is that the opposite is also true: the way you use your breath impacts your mental, physical and emotional state. Given that it is much simpler to regulate your breathing than it is all the thoughts and emotions inside you, learning how to control it will become a great ally of yours.

In this part, we are going to see how to increase your energy through the way you breathe. I usually call this type of breathing Power Breathing.

You will be breathing in through your nose and out through your mouth. When you breathe in, do so quickly; when you breathe out, add some resistance (usually making a 's' or 'sh' sound will help you) so that breathing out will last longer. After eight or nine of these breaths, you will feel that your body is increasing its level of energy, and some of the worrying thoughts you had in mind are no longer present. If while exhaling you imagine your fears too are being pushed away, the effect will be even stronger, but the sole fact you are breathing in this way will already raise your energy level.

Body

The other thing that is easier to manage than your thoughts and emotions is the movement of your body. Before your performance, find a moment to move your body, by jumping (the loo is often the best place for this) or taking a brisk walk. Smiling (with both your mouth and eyes) will also help. It does not matter if, in that moment, you feel like doing anything but smiling. When you smile, your body releases the same hormones that it does when you are happy, and this will make you feel better.

Relaxation then

If it is true that before the performance you need to increase your energy to be ready to face anything, there may be a moment during the performance itself in which your stress and fears pop up again—especially if that is what you have been used to for your whole life.

In that moment there are two techniques that will make a huge difference.

Breathe

We saw how breathing can help you to increase your energy. If you use it well, it can also help you to lower your heartrate and decrease tension when you feel nervous. Out of all the relaxing breathing techniques that I have experienced, there is one that has struck me the most, as it is fast to apply, unnoticeable, and effective. I call it the Chilled Breathing technique.

You will be breathing in and out using only your nose. If, while breathing in through your nose, you were asked to tap where you felt that breath goes, you would probably tap the sides of your nose, or the top. For this kind of breathing, however, you instead need to 'push' your breath towards your throat. Instead of it going up as it would usually do, I imagine it going towards the back. Once you understand what movement this is, it is very simple to realise. It also helps if you place a hand on your belly, making sure that, when you inhale in that way, your belly expands. Breathing out will be a natural consequence, and as long as you do it from your nose there are no specific directions.

When you do three to four of these breaths, you can feel your body relaxing, releasing the tension. By the way, this kind of breathing can be done at any time, not only before your performance! It is soothing, relaxing, and fast.

Get tenser and tenser

There is another technique that a lot of our clients find very helpful as a way to release the tension they feel before a speech, an exam, an interview or any kind of performance: the Full Body Tension.

When you are nervous, some parts of your body become tense. Even though you may not often realise it, this micro-tension affects your performance. The Full Body Tension is a great way to get rid of it.

The first step is to create tension throughout your whole body by contracting every muscle you can. (Making a fist with both hands will help too.) Once you feel that you are tensed, hold onto this contraction for a few moments and then release all of it.

The reason why this works so well is that if it can be extremely hard to otherwise identify all of your the micro-tensions in order to release them, and so by forcefully contracting your entire body you will catch all of those areas that had some micro-tension, and you will feel much more relaxed. And again, this technique can be applied unnoticeably.

Words: 1,124   *Time (in seconds):* _____

CHAPTER TWENTY-ONE

Presentation Is Key

[Bed is fine]

Managing your emotional state in order to perform at your best is a great tool to have in your arsenal, and most of the time it will be enough for you to showcase your preparation.

However, refining the way you express concepts will make it almost impossible for people not to notice how many things you know. Whether it is an interview or a presentation for your manager, you can imagine how important it is not to underestimate this aspect.

We could write a whole book (or more than one) solely on the art of presenting. Here I do not want to go into the details of a perfect public speaking technique (which you can find in any blog, and which are far more effective when taught in a practical way), but instead focus on some techniques you can apply in order to deliver your knowledge effectively. The reality is that people often make the huge mistake of focusing their energy on the technicalities of public speaking. These definitely have an impact, but are only one aspect of it.

If I had to narrow down what makes a presentation effective regardless of the context in which you are, I would say that there are two areas and six sub-areas you need to master:

Preparing:
- How aligned your presentation is with its goal
- How clear your presentation is
- How big your iceberg is

Presenting:
- How well you remember your presentation
- How well you manage your nerves
- How engaging you are in the delivery

If you look at these six requirements, you will notice that most of them are already part of your arsenal if you have read the book from start to finish. If you have not, do not worry. I am going to direct you to the main parts you need to learn in order to become a great presenter.

Words: 311   Time (in seconds): _____

Preparing
{Easy Peasy layer}

One goal, different strategies

One mistake I notice many people make when presenting is that they just start sharing everything they know on the topic; doing so without first asking themselves the most important question: What is my goal in this communication? This applies both when you have the time and the opportunity to sit down and prepare your speech, and when you are asked something on the spot and need to improvise your answer.

To help you narrow down your options when seeking to clarify your communication goals, there are four purposes your communication could have: inform, entertain, inspire and persuade (at times it will be a mixture of all of them).

Even when you are there to inform, the goal of your informing will always be different. You may want to show the good work you have done; you may want your manager to be concerned about a project that is not proceeding as expected; you may want to motivate someone; you may want to negotiate your salary; you may want to entertain your listeners, or to educate them. In any case, you want to elicit an emotion (and consequent action) from your listener. Even the most boring presentation on paper will have a completely different effect if you start by asking yourself: what is my goal in this communication?

I did this with one of our Genius Mentees who was preparing a one-hour presentation for the stakeholders of a very important bank. Initially he was planning to inform them on the progress of each project. But merely 'informing' people is never a good choice. So he asked himself 'What is my goal?', and realised that his real goal was not only to let them know which projects were going ahead better than expected and which ones were stuck, but to show them all the measures that had been taken to restart the stuck projects, and (most importantly for him) to discover whether it was possible to increase the budget.

Starting from that awareness, we restructured his presentation in a way that was aligned with his goal. And guess what happened? They agreed to increase the budget, and were vociferously impressed by his honesty and initiative.

Whether it is a one-minute pitch or a multiple-day convention, if you do not have a clear goal you will end up informing your listeners rather than communicating an emotion that will lead to an action.

The clearer the concept, the clearer the expression

Do you know anyone who knows a lot of things, but when you listen to them you cannot seem to be able to follow their train of thought? Remember: presenting what you have learned or worked on is about *the listener*, not about the speaker. You need to make sure you express the ideas that you have in your mind in the easiest way possible, always making sure that it is aligned with the goal you have selected.

There are two elements you need to pay attention to: the overall structure, and the way you explain concepts.

Clear Structure

The structure needs to be tailored to both the purpose of your communication and the type of audience you have. There are several templates that can help you structure your speech according to your goal, and I will suggest some reading later. Regardless of the nature and length of the speech, however, some principles are universal.

In order to receive something, you need to give something.

If you want to get something from your communication, be ready to give. Give value, entertainment, information, emotions, something. You are there to give, and when your listeners see how much you are giving, they will be more willing to give back.

Focusing on what you want to give will also greatly help your nerves. The first time I found myself talking in front of a thousand people, I felt myself getting a bit nervous before starting. I had never had so many people in front of me at once, and the kind of interaction and contact with the audience would be very different from what I was used to. In that moment, right before going on stage, I had a realisation. Nervousness was coming from my focus on how *they* would react, how much *they* would enjoy it, what *they* would decide to do at the end of the speech. 'Giulia', I told myself, 'You are here to *give*. If anything else happens, that will be a consequence. You do not have control on how *they* will like it, but you can definitely control what *you* will give.' My nervousness disappeared, and guess how the event went? People loved it, and I got tens of thousands of pounds' worth of business out of it.

What can you give to the person or people in front of you?

Breaking the ice at the beginning will make the situation warmer.

If you want people to be warm to your proposal, to you, to your work—to anything—you must break the ice. This does not always entail cracking a joke or being funny, as this will depend on the context of the conversation. But you need to instil in the listener an empathy towards you: by finding common ground; by letting them understand your honest intentions; or even just by smiling. At times the ice can be thick, as the situation is tense and therefore you require something strong to break it. Other times you are presenting your knowledge or your ideas to a warmer audience of friends, family and/or supporters. But regardless of whether you are communicating with a thousand strangers, your stakeholders, your teammates or your other half, if you do not break the ice then your communication may not have the desired effect on its audience.

If you do not ask, you may not receive.

Some people know that they should give a lot when presenting, but hope the simple act of giving will be enough in order for them to receive something in return. Wrong. If you wish to receive, you need to ask for whatever it is you want. Do not be scared of asking. In most contexts, people already expect you to ask. In the remaining ones, it is only by asking that you allow them to give. According to the kind of presentation, you may state your request at the beginning ('Today, I want you to learn…'; 'Today I want you to laugh like never before'; and so on), or at the end ('This is why I am asking you to…'), and at times you may insert your ask both at the beginning and the end ('My goal for today is for you to…' and 'This is why I am asking you to…').

Remember that every context is different, but in almost all of them asking will be part of the process.

Your talk is like a flight: take off, cruise, landing.

If you want to present effectively, you cannot ramble randomly. You need to structure your talk—regardless of it being impromptu or planned, short or long—so that the listener can easily follow the thread of what you are saying.

At the beginning, state what you will say (take off), then say it (cruise), and then say what you have just said (landing). Of course, this generic structure leaves a lot of space for creative license. You may decide to inject more suspense by seeding a reference to something you will later talk about; or you could develop your cruise phase through a Hero's Journey structure and in that case, during the takeoff, you may not go into details but just inform people that you will tell them a story. You can play with it, choosing what to say and how to say it in order to keep your audience engaged and, in turn, reach your goal (inform, entertain, inform or persuade).

Using mind maps to create your speech will work wonders both in terms of clarity and easiness of memorisation (see Chapter Thirteen—passage on Mind Maps).

Clear Explanation

You will be able to communicate something clearly in the moment in which that thought will be clear in your mind. Whenever people tell me 'It's clear in my head, but I do not know how to express it', I know that one thing is for certain: they have not done enough practice of step two of the Hourglass Technique—explaining the concept to a child (Chapter Eleven).

No one is to blame for this. All of us process concepts in our mind according to different learning styles, and one such style is called Wholist vs Analytic—which represents whether you process information as a whole (wholist) or broken down into components (analytic). Do you know anyone who cannot help talking about all the details of a situation? And someone who has the 1,000-yard perspective but struggles to pay attention to what is happening underneath their nose? This depends on your learning style, and will affect not only how you picture the information but also how you express it to the external world.

Unless you learn how to moderate your style—using the strengths that it offers and avoiding the obstacles you may incur—you will tend to favour your default style, to the detriment of those who differ from you.

Remember the Hourglass Technique? When you start processing the information better, it will be very easy for you to unravel your thoughts and explain them with clarity, regardless of your default style. Your listeners will appreciate this 'gift' immensely, as it is not that common for people to explain things clearly; yet you will know that it is probably not a gift, but instead a skill that you have developed and that everyone can improve.

As one of our Genius in 21 Days clients, Kuldip, said: 'I cannot believe how much clearer my thoughts are since I took Genius in 21

Days! I have learned how to think in a way that is more structured and much clearer.'

Iceberg

What are icebergs a symbol of? They represent all that is underneath the surface and that which makes the tip visible. When you are presenting, your iceberg is one of the foremost elements, but it is often the one people just do not have the time to focus on, and that they therefore, mistakenly, leave out.

The concept is simple: you need to know much more than you share. The reasons why building a strong iceberg will make a huge difference are manifold for one thing, the more you know, the more confident you will feel, and confidence plays a huge role in how your message will come across; equally, if your listener had questions or curiosities about the topic, you want to be able to answer these promptly, as this will showcase your preparation and increase your leadership.

Just a couple of weeks ago, I ran a webinar on Time Management. Immediately following the webinar, of the participants texted a member of my team to share how amazed he was at the webinar itself, and especially at my ability to answer promptly any kind of question attendees had.

Only if your iceberg is strong can you answer quickly and accurately. And you can only create a strong iceberg by putting in the time to research, read, study, deepen topics, and—in certain scenarios—apply.

So, what is the best way to increase your iceberg on a topic? Applying everything you have read in this book!

If this is the first section you are reading of the book, start with how to become a more efficient reader, as most of the material you will find on a topic will come from articles and books you read (see Chapter Eight—passages on Reading).

Words: 1,974   *Time (in seconds):* _____

Presenting
{Easy Peasy layer}

Memory

To be a great presenter you need to remember what you want to say. This should go without saying, but I still see many people running presentations reading their notes all the time.

Of course, according to the kind of presentation, you may have some slides or notes. But what do you think will be more engaging: constantly looking at your notes, or looking at your listeners?

Remembering things properly allows you to show more confidence because you feel more confident! It allows you to look at whoever is listening, so that you can pick up on how they are feeling about what you are saying. It allows you to answer questions confidently, without losing your train of thought. It allows you to adjust what you want to say, according to what the people in front of you need.

There will be presentations (usually short pitches) that you want to know almost by heart, while for others it will be enough for you to memorise the logical structure of your talk and possibly some details (especially in the way you want to take off and land). According to how detailed you want to be, you will use different memorisation strategies. Very often, using the Velcro Palace will turn out to be your favourite, as it makes it very easy to recall the information you need at a stage when your nerves are conspiring to work against you (see Chapter Sixteen—Memory Palace).

Nerves

Although some people may find you cute if you are nervous when presenting your ideas, in most cases nerves will not serve your cause. It is fundamental to learn how to feel more at ease, because it will help you to focus your attention on what really matters: making sure that your message comes across.

I will not spend any words on this, as you can find all you need to know a few pages back (see Chapter Twenty—Peak Performance). Become more comfortable, and your presentations will immediately improve—even if you do not apply anything else! It is not enough in its own, but it is that single factor that, if improved, will make the biggest difference.

Becoming engaging

Once everything else is in place, it becomes a matter of learning some techniques to improve your technical delivery of what you want to say. As I mentioned before, a lot of books have been written on the subject; and, even more importantly, I believe the best way to improve your delivery comes from practising with someone who is able to give you some constructive feedback.

There will be some elements you want to focus on especially, and at times even just acknowledging these will help you improve instantaneously.

Are you able to adjust your tone according to the message you want to convey? How much emphasis do you place on the pauses you make? Do you fill every silent gap with a filler word ('Hmm', 'OK', 'You know', lengthened words)? How much do you adjust your pace to align with what you are saying?

Whether you are talking to one or a thousand people, all these elements will make a huge difference in how your message will come across. Practise any time you can, learn how to play with your voice, observe the reactions people have when you use a strategic pause instead of a filler word. If all the other points are not in place, this will not be enough; but, when all the other points are taken care of, this will move the needle in the direction of mastery.

Words: 597   Time (in seconds): _____

CONCLUSION

BEGINNING

When I think about all the techniques taught in this book, the first word that comes to mind is Freedom. That is what they have given me and thousands of other people. It is true that, to experience the feeling of Freedom at its fullest power, you need to apply and practise, which may initially take time. But as I was telling you at the beginning of this journey, just applying all the No Effort and Easy Peasy techniques has already enhanced your learning power and taken you to levels you never imagined. You may go back to that initial list you ticked and notice that you have already acquired more tools that you expected, but in fact the journey starts now, with your next goals to reach and your next growth to target.

I believe Freedom is a word that carries with it a lot of power, and that goes hand in hand with learning. Fredrick Douglass said, 'Once you learn, you will be forever free', and I do not think he was far off!

> Freedom is recognising that your limitations were there only because you had not yet learned how to walk past them.
>
> It is embracing fears instead of running away from them, to learn what they can teach you.
>
> It is realising that your true potential is revealed when you remove all the excess—fears, doubt, anger—because it does not serve you anymore.
>
> It is looking at yourself with that scientific mind we have mentioned so many times: to observe

your thoughts, emotions and actions; and to improve what needs to be improved, instead of judging what is not yet as you would like it to be.

It is choosing what you want to do in your life not according to what you think you can do but according to what you really want for yourself.

It is having the courage and the means to pursue your passions and become an expert in them.

It is having the power to learn what you need from a situation or a book to get closer to the person you want to be or the goals you want to achieve.

Being able to learn like a 'Genius' allows you to do all of this. Now you have removed a lot of preconceptions about what you can or cannot do. There may be some techniques you have already been able to apply effectively from the moment you read them in this book, and there may be others you would like to go over again. Use your talents to improve your weaknesses: understand what you are a natural at and use it to improve everything else. Too often we are accustomed to focusing on what we are not able to do rather than what we are capable of.

Always aim for perfection but never expect it, which means always strive to be better and to learn something new, but know that you will never achieve perfection—because, as soon as you feel you've reached it, you will go back to square one of a new level, in the never ending game of life.

Of all the strategies and techniques I have shared in this book, if there is one message I would like to stick in your mind it is that when you cannot do something yet, it does not mean you will not be able to do it at all. In most cases, it will be a matter of breaking it down into things you need to learn, applying what this book teaches you and then observing how your world changes. As Julian Barnes put it, 'The more you learn, the less you fear.'

I hope to hear about your results, small or big as they may seem, because every single step carries with it the effort, the passion, the dream; the person you are and the one you will be. Sharing them with someone else means acknowledging them, bringing them to life and giving them the strength to become the stepping-stone for what comes next.

I hope to meet you soon, Genius by Choice.

Inspiration Time from Our Genius Alumni

I am currently studying Management Information System at Ashesi University in Ghana.

Before Genius, I was an above average student, but my time management was horrendous, and my attention span was pretty low. I was still getting a few A's, B's and the occasional C in my academics but I wanted to be exceptional. I wanted to become organized and read more and learn even more. So, after the course I focused on speed reading and memorization. I set goals for myself which I over-exceeded. One such goal was to learn 20 bible verses in 2 weeks. I ended up learning 50 bible verses in less than 24 hours. My mentor kept pushing me and I kept breaking past limits I thought I had.

I decided to take the course not only to be the best version of myself, but also to invest into the life I knew I wanted. Without this course, I may have never unearthed all my potential.

When the pandemic started, even though the quarantine disoriented me, I focused on learning and applying the techniques I had acquired from G21D. I eventually got 100% in my final exam.

In addition to that, I saw an opportunity for a Facebook Mentorship. It has been a dream of mine to work with Facebook, but I wasn't the best programmer.

Given the tools I now have, I decided that, regardless of my skill, I would learn what I could. Therefore, I set a 2-week goal to study coding to get ready for the Facebook Hackathon.

I applied the G21D learning strategies and time management techniques throughout my preparatory process. I eventually finished the 2-hour hacker project in about 1 hour and 15 minutes and I scored 40/42. Aftermath, Facebook accepted me into a 13-week mentorship session and I got direct access to the final stage of the 2021 Internship track!

Toby Woode - University Student

YOUR A-Z HANDBOOK

A
Assessment (Read)
Applications (Memorise)

B
Boosters (Read)

C
Cycles (Prepare)
Cover (Read)
Critical Reading (Read)

D
Decide (Prepare)
Dream up (Priming)

E
Estimate (Prepare)
End (Prepare)

F
Focus (Prepare)
Flow (Prepare)

G
Goal (Read)

H
Hooks (Memorise)

I
Investigate (Prepare)

J
Journal (Prepare)

K
Killers (Prepare)
Keywords (Internalise)

L
Label (Internalise)
Lock (Memorise)
Lists (Memorise)
Long Term (Memorise)

M
Memory Palace (Memorise)

N
New Information (Memorise)
Numbers (Memorise)

O
Organising (Internalise)

P
Preview (Read)
Processing (Internalise)

Peak Performance (Express)
Present With Confidence (Express)

Q
Questions (Read)

R
Revisit (Prepare)

S
Scheduled (Prepare)
Skimming (Read)
Scanning (Read)

T
Trigger (Memorise)

U
Understand (Internalise)

V
Velcro (Memorise)
Visualise (Memorise)

W
Welcome (Priming)

X
Experiment (Prepare)

Y
Your Study Sanctuary (Prepare)

Z
Zoom (Internalise)

ACKNOWLEDGEMENTS

Writing a book is a lengthy process, as it starts not with the first word you type on your file but with the journey to acquire the knowledge you will share with your readers: whether or not you already know that you will commit it to paper.

There are so many people that have contributed to this book—either by taking tangible actions or by being part of a never-ending journey that started in 2008—and my heart is filled with gratitude for the support everyone has given me.

To my wonderful partner, Yaw, who never seems to get bored of showing his support: whether by bringing in new ideas, vetting mine or enlightening me with a point of view I have not yet considered.

To Mum, Dad, Stefano, Marco, Ilenia and Laura (and Simona, Luca, Mattia, Carlo, Enrico, Emanuela and Dana) for being close to me no matter the distance. Stefano is the real trigger for why this book came to life now rather than later: one day he told me 'We should expand this Eleven Tips brochure', and now here we are, 55,000 words later.

To the whole Genius in 21 Days team, particularly to Luca Lorenzoni, extraordinary mentor and friend; Massimo De Donno, constant source of inspiration; Giacomo Navone, who some time ago suggested I write a book; Stefano Vecchi, who was the first Instructor I learned from; Eva Albertinazzi, always ready to lend an ear when I needed to verbalise my ideas about the book; and all the other Instructors who share our mission to make people fall in love with learning again, and who relentlessly teach these techniques and live by everything that Genius in 21 Days is every single day.

To my closest team in London, Accra and New Jersey. Yaw, Martina, Clara, Michela, Giulia, Zachin, Kuldip, Carol and Delasi: the trust you have placed in my dream fuels me with energy every day, and I am so grateful and honoured to be playing on the same team. A special mention goes to Clara for drawing the illustrations. And also to all the next generation of Genius Mentors: training you is a pure joy, and has been a driver for many parts of the book.

To all the people who, upon hearing of this project, asked how they could help. From small to huge tasks, you have helped this book come to life.

To Irem Khan, not only for being the amazing friend that she is, but for building a website in record time to allow all the readers to download the blueprints and book their free surprise gift.

To Richard Arcus, wonderful editor: you did not just help me phrase concepts in better English, but you also managed to make me laugh a lot while doing it. That's the spirit!

To everyone at the Self-Publishing School, who helped clarify how to bridge the gap between writing a book and publishing a book. Your resources are precious, and your coaches very dedicated (thank you Scott Allan).

To Imran Shaikh, wonderful designer: in a contest alongside almost six hundred designs, two of your covers went to the final three, which speaks volumes of your quality.

Last but not least, to you, the reader. I do not know your face, but I did imagine it at every page I was writing. You have been my North Star, guiding me in every choice I had to make. The topic is very complex, and my leitmotif was 'What will make the journey of the reader easier?' And so a big final thank you goes to you!

REFERENCES

This book comes from years and years spent studying and researching. While writing it, I didn't consult any book, but the only reason for that is because I've been consulting them for years. To be honest, the biggest 'book' has been written by the thousands of people who I have had the pleasure of working with: every question has been a reason to find new solutions, at times by studying more, other times by creating something new.

In this section, I will mention some of the actual books that have had an influence on me in terms of learning, in the event you want to deepen your knowledge and read some of them. After all, now you know how to do it quickly!

Prepare:
- Dweck, Carol, *Mindset: Changing The Way You Think To Fulfil Your Potential*

Read:
- Buzan, Tony, *The Speed Reading Book: Read more, learn more, achieve more*
- Scheele, R. Paul: *PhotoReading*

Internalise:
- Buzan, Tony, *The Mind Map Book: Unlock your creativity, boost your memory, change your life*

Memorise:
- Buzan, Tony, *The Memory Book: How to remember anything you want*
- Foer, Joshua, *Moonwalking with Einstein*

Express:
- Anderson, Chris, TED Talks: The official TED guide to public speaking
- Gallo, Carmine, *Talk Like TED: The 9 Public Speaking Secrets of the World's Top Minds*
- Voss, Chris, *Never Split the Difference: Negotiating as if Your Life Depended on It*

The brain and overall learning:
- Magrini, Marco, *The Brain: A User's Manual: A simple guide to the world's most complex machine*
- Dispenza, Joe, *Evolve Your brain: The Science of Changing Your Mind*
- Buzan, Tony, *Use Your Head: How to unleash the power of your mind*

For those of you who speak Italian:
- Bartoletti, Alessandro, *Lo studente strategico: Come risolvere rapidamente i problemi di studio (Italian Edition)*
- Lorenzoni, Luca, Navone, Giacomo, et al., *Fenomeno in 21 giorni: Il metodo esclusivo per potenziare al massimo la tua mente nel lavoro, nello studio, nelle sfide (Italian Edition)*
- Navone, Giacomo and De Donno, Massimo, *Genio in 21 giorni: i segreti dell'efficienza mentale: tecniche di memoria, lettura veloce, mappe mentali e strategie di apprendimento avanzato (Italian Edition)*
- Oliverio, Alberto, *L'arte di ricordare. La memoria e i suoi segreti (Italian Edition)*

www.ingramcontent.com/pod-product-compliance
Lightning Source LLC
LaVergne TN
LVHW041625060526
838200LV00040B/1447